MW01234510

"I AM..."
Experidigmer

Living the Joy Equation

MARK GRACE

ISBN: 978-0-98489-988-3 (print)
ISBN: 978-0-98489-989-0 (ebook)

CONTENTS

PART 1:
Consciousness Context

PART 2:
Infinite Joy

PART 3:
Connected Life

PART 4:
Healing – No Walls

PART 5:
Rules of Experidigm Economy

PART 6:
Path of Life

PART 7:
Education Needed

PART 8:
Living Experidigm Life

PART 9:
Evolving

APPENDIX:

Acknowledgements

Disclaimer

Dear Reader:

This book contains information, suggestions, and opinions about improving discussion in groups, companies and among the status quo. The use, misuse, understanding, or misunderstanding of the material, in whole or in part, is the sole responsibility of the reader.

Neither the publisher nor the authors assume responsibility or liability, jointly or individually, to any person, group, organization, or entity regarding any emotional or material loss, damage, or injury caused or alleged to be caused directly or indirectly by the information contained in this book.

Readers are advised to use this material in a safe and logical manner. In some cases, the material is most effective when used in conjunction with professional legal and/or consulting services.

All examples and references to behavior in companies and of people are only illustrative and not based on any actual company or person.

Mark Grace

SYNOPSIS

Connected experidigmers soar. Just say NEXT, and more Pointing After choices come and more selections are made. Joy is received in the flow of the experidigm and the connections.

We visualize. We choose. We experience. We reach higher. Again and again. We capture the kingdom. Have you experienced "I am...?" The sheer joy of being in an "I am..." experience, the experience you created connected to your joy in that moment? Yes, you own and you create experiences, which can be the joy of the Infinite or an earthly hell. You decide. You choose. You make the selections to have joy with all your experiences. You keep choosing and evolving to your highest level of experience—no one can stop you, but you. Your free will lets you choose. Keep choosing to move to higher and higher levels, to more and more joy.

A major reason for living is to create joy in your personal experiences connected to other joyful people. The Joy equation focuses on what is most important to receive joy and what to avoid:

$$\text{Joy} = (\Sigma \text{ experidigms}) \times (\# \text{ connections}) - \Sigma \text{TTers}$$

Focus on creating new experidigms with the support of other "I am..." creative people connections. Creating experidigms and learning how to connect can be taught in school. With enough experidigmers, an economy of value sharing through cooperation can flourish. The focus on experidigms point the way up the Path of Life and attracts joy and love and the Infinite "I am...." Avoid Turd Throwers (TTers) who will try to stop experidigms and connections. Turd throwers prevent joy.

NEXT: "I Am...." Experidigmer declares the simple Joy equation of life and captures that joy every day. See how to design and live future "big-picture" experiences called Experidigms while connecting with others for contributions. Determine who you are, where you are going with your "I am...ness," and why share with others. Everyone should have experidigms to share.

A STORY
NEXT

Life is a big sandbox, and I have fun playing in the sandbox. I build anything I can imagine, like sandcastles, and then I build the NEXT sandcastle of my dreams. Sometimes Turd Throwers or Takers kick and knock over my creations, but I just make a new one, and do the NEXT thing.

I have learned to picture all components coming together, and then see the various rearrangements, choose new components to add, and move forward and make the experience happen. I see the components come together (and they always do), and then I see improvements needed, and they are added. This visualization just keeps going on and on, adding and adding, I just do more choosing and doing. If I see obstacles, I go another way, making new choices to make the experience.

I smile. My earliest memories are about poking things, to instigate and see what happens. Walking along a creek bed, I would use my sturdy walking stick to poke at bugs and animals under the rock I turned over. Wow, I would see an alien world of life and activity, new and foreign to anything I had seen before. Clearly, there are other worlds out there to explore. As I grew, books and experts poked at my brain opening up so many possible experiences (work, play, travel, eating exotic food, etc.) and ways of learning (books, subjects, music, art, acting, doing, sporting, etc.). However, getting stuck happens, and becoming mired in the status quo happens, resulting in complacency and stagnation. Being connected with different types of people cause new connections, sharing and combining of unrelated ways and modes of thinking help you escape from complacency. Escape limits. I know I have no limits if my mind can "visualize" it. If I can visualize it, I can create it, and make it happen, make it real. Do it, then say "NEXT." Visualize the "pointing after" NEXT and do. I always add to what exists, then build on it with NEXT, pointing upward.

My essence and life is different than poking around, being inquisitive, and questioning the nature of things. Nor is it only about searching. No, my essence is a visualizing-seeing-doing thing, and experiencing the joy of the experience. Picture learning what is now, trying it, adding to it, and then seeing what is NEXT, and trying to build it and share it. It could be better experienced more fully with other perspectives. Then build on that. Combine share, integrate, evolve – always looking at NEXT, with love. Not just seeing differently, not just seeing from my perspective, and moving toward that; not about satisfaction or dissatisfaction, or really any emotion at all, except joy. Just experiencing NEXT and sharing it and learning from it.

Life is more like viewing a line of experiences waiting for the individual to pay attention to them. There is always a NEXT. The NEXT vision always steps into the front of the infinite NEXT line. I realize the NEXT waiting line goes on forever, so I never run out of NEXT. Creating and doing bring some form of joy. It is like the anticipation and joy of turning over the rock and seeing the surprise that is there. Life is that way, one transition to the NEXT transition, and the many smiles along the way.

Joy is not about success. Joy is living in the NEXT experience, knowing there are many more to come. Realistically, sometimes obstacles cloud my vision of the Pointing After experidigm as to what would be NEXT; sometimes, fear and doubt creep in to convince me the line was not there, but, these delusional issues, solely created in my mind, do not change the fact that the NEXT line is always there. NEXT!!! And so NEXT comes again, and again. You know there is a tomorrow, and tomorrow contains NEXT.

The more NEXT experiences I have, the more my mind opens up; therefore, the more NEXTs I can visualize. I know if I limit my experiences, I limit me—that is just stupid. Why would I want to limit me?

I live my time, not someone else's status quo marketed to me that seem nice, but really are not. Picturing futures and trying them is my favorite learning experience. Obstacles do not exist in my infinite line of NEXT; I just say NEXT and move on. This is much different than goal setting and having an obstacle block the road to that goal. The obstacle is made real by the "realness" of my self-inflicted goal. I change the goal, and just create other self-inflicted obstacles and related new goals. I change my NEXT and I will find new learning and new opportunities to live my NEXT life. Here are some examples of comparing goals versus experiences:

1) Good grades versus learning,

2) Material things versus caring,

3) Sex versus love,

4) Seeking attention versus "I am...ness" and we-ness".

My NEXT experience is not me alone. If I share my line of NEXT experiences with others, and they share their NEXT line with me, I now have double the NEXT lines I can witness and/or share the doing with others. Connected, I have the stick poking me to the NEXT experience. The poker may be my friend or the NEXT experience wanting me. OK, sounds great, but some people are hurtful and they hide and blow up NEXT, so I get away from these obstacles as people, and new positive resources appear as I try to keep focus on that NEXT. Is it really worth it to live with obstacles to hold you in place when there are an infinite more NEXT? I build on what NEXT is for me and share with others and go to the NEXT with fewer obstacles.

Mark Grace

I have never understood why we have the "rags to riches" worship culture that values overcoming big obstacles to be who they are, and then they wear that as a badge of courage. We glorify the struggle, and say it is worth it. The result is not the culmination of one's life. Even after success, there is always NEXT. Otherwise I am "dead in place." I choose to walk on, so walk with me to NEXT--it does not have to be a struggle against obstacles.

In my work there has always been NEXT. Each one adding something new and enlightening to the NEXT transition. Even though work might have been viewed by others as a series of successes, I do not view it that way. New experiences paved the way to more experiences to reach higher and higher levels of understanding and experience. Each time I set goals, I reached them, many times reaching the goal was somehow hollow, giving me the scary feeling that I was done and finished. I do not like that feeling. So, beyond goal setting is the NEXT experience. Yes, work has NEXT experiences filled with learning and joy. Here is a brief review of some of my NEXTs starting from my first work days:

+ Telling jokes on group rides at amusement park

+ Offering expert advice on finishing home improvement projects for homeowners

+ Running hospital blood tests and reporting results to help heal patients

+ Making new chemical formulations to deliver value to processing plants

+ Stewarding operational performance for the world's largest company

+ Launching global chemical company with partners and revolutionizing customer experience to control usage

+ Leading technology development employees to improve global manufacturing & product quality

+ Creating and selling my first company focused on making food better

+ Participating in creating the "smart" grid

+ Believing that by improving communication with visuals all will lead a better life, so I built visual talking for all

+ Participating in enabling anyone to build Alive Spaces where they select-live-refresh their space to match their needs and functions

+ Visualizing how anyone can create his or her perfect experidigms

In my social life, each NEXT added to my increased joy. Each social NEXT just keeps adding to each other:

+ Playing at sports

+ Playing outdoors, camping, and sleeping in RV

+ Learning anywhere I can

+ Getting married

+ Raising kids

+ Travelling the world spreading news

+ Teaching innovation and creativity

+ Loving everybody for their uniqueness

+ Caring about what I play at and with whom

The only commonalty with these experidigms is that they were part of a stream and flow of NEXTs, not fully planned, as uncontrollable change demanded a new NEXT.

My connectedness to others and their many NEXT lines has dramatically grown the NEXT lines waiting for me to choose them.

I sit here looking over fall foliage at a small lake, smiling with the beauty of all the NEXT transitions around me: leaves changing colors and falling everywhere; animals rustling in the leaves; fish jumping in the water; insects buzzing around. There is movement everywhere, everywhere the essence says NEXT, with no judgment, only the expectation of NEXT.

What's NEXT? I just picture it and do it and a new NEXT appears, and if I do not like that NEXT, I choose from the infinite number of NEXTs waiting in line for me. They say, "Pick me!" NEXT! Walk with me.

FOREWORD
No Box – Free Will

No matter who, what, where, when, how, why, whose, which, or any other question, one thing is for sure -- all humans have free will. There are no bonds or boundaries to birth free will, except if one individual chooses to give up portions or all of free will. Free will is not lost; we choose to use it or not. Free will is directed by each person. Free will follows what the person points upward for and moves toward. This book is about what to direct free will toward in the given space suit of a body. Sure the space suit might be limited by the laws of physics; however, free will is creative and can create infinite possibilities. Free will can point up to any potential, and make it happen. The key observation in this book is to keep pointing and acting toward a visualized experidigm. Each person has free will "I am…" that creates and connects to the Infinite 'I am….'"

The target to point to for using this space suit here on earth is joy. Yes, joy can be experienced and created by "I am…" free will. By evolving the experience, joy will evolve as well, avoiding stagnation or addiction. To get outside any constraining box placed on free will, sharing and connecting with other "I am…ers" will get joy and lead to evolving joy. Life is that simple. Focus on positive experience. Point up. No thing will ever stop you from your experience and Joy equation.

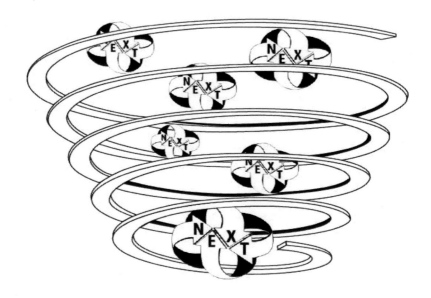

No thing has power over you. Be careful though. Some people will be false partners and point to false experiences. For example, a false, spineless leader may say "you can be a partner if you work hard for a long time, earn your stripes, and beat out the others". Of course, as one believes they are the strongest and invincible, he or she points to this false experidigm, and defers joy to get "partner" in the future. Not so for the vast majority. Living in a false experidigm enslaved to another taking-human being is limiting and a waste of time. Only choose for your experidigm that which is bigger than any box. False partner visions come in many shapes and sizes. We will look at some later. Beware of being defined and categorized by someone else. That is the first step others use to put your "I am…ness" in a box and take your creativity for them. No thing can take your "I am…." Be careful with TTers, Takers and false partners.

INTRODUCTION
Exploring I Am

Just say, "I am…." Allowing "I am…" is the greatest joy in life. Individual free will allows "I am…." Free will allows only what we want into our minds and we then believe what we want. In our allowing, we enable "I am…." We are self-aware, not selfish or materialistic, and connected to all Infinite "I am…."

The real question is -- what do we allow in our minds to create the "I am…?" The "I am…" Infinite is already in our mind and through the "I am…" Infinite we can allow anything in our mind. We are in control of what we let into our mind. What we let in and what we think are within our control, but this control can be lost by what we let in and what we think (sounds a bit circular, but can be just like the fox that we let into the hen house). What we allow in is crucial to who we are now or at any time in our life. What we allow in makes our reality and further attracts the things to match and keep our reality. It is very important to manage and restrict what we allow in to our goodness and joy.

Unfortunately, when we are born, or as we go through life, very few people, (including family, figureheads, religions, schools, work, or friends) tell us that "so as you let in and then think, so you are." As a blank slate, we let in our minds those around us who keep saying "you are…fill in the blank…" and we begin to resemble their "you are…" and structure our thinking and resultant reality around their "you are…" scripting. Some might say,

"You are a liar," so lying is let into the brain forever, unless it is purposely deflected away. If let in, we become a liar.

If their "you are..." is negative, like "you are stupid," or "you can't learn," or "you can't play this or that", then you might give up on these things and become something less than you could be. Or, you hear TV ads or social media language that say drink this party alcohol or the friends say "let's get drunk," and you go drinking and lose your "I am...." You willfully create your own internal "you are..." world created by those around you and by advertising. Once this is let in, there is no real "I am..." or any real connection to the Infinite "I am...." It is time to scream at the top of your lungs, "I am...," and "I will be..." and I experience and I choose...."

If others promote a "you are..." that is positive, like "You are a genius: be a doctor," or "you are a great athlete," or "you sing and dance so well," then you could have a strong desire (supported by friends) to become that and be as they say, "You are great...fill in the blank...." So you become as they say. Although this seems "better" than a negative "you are...," the fact is you are still being someone else's "you are...." Maybe this good "you are..." is your "I am...:" only you can tell. If you become stagnant or addicted, it is a "you are...," not an "I am...."

We exist to be "I am...," not a "you are...." There is continuous joy in "I am..." and joy in the connections with the "I am..." Infinite and others who are "I am...." There is only temporary joy with the satisfaction of a "you are...." "You are..." may only please or placate another for a short time. "I am..." is your foundation. "I am..." is the supporting rock from which all joy flows. The "I am..." is being continually built and added to and flowing to better and more joy. "I am..." is part of, captures, and journeys with all infinity and all possibilities. Each knowing visualization and related experidigm adds to your "I am...." In *Choosing Up*, we discussed experidigms and how connected with others you can grow your experiences. Your connected growth is an "I am..." growth. You have selectively let in and made your choices to be "I am..." and to grow your "I am...." In *TTers Beware* we talked about how others prevent you and take from your "I am...."

"I am..." creates joy. Joy is a direct result from connecting with the "I am..." Infinite and other "I am...ers" through experiences you let in. How you live in your "I am..." creates joy. This book is all about the relationship between your joy and your experidigms and living your experidigms with greatest joy. You create and let in your "I am...." You are also solely in charge of preventing "you are..." and complacency from covering up or destroying your "I am...." The only experience that is real to you is that which you let into your 'I am....' Poverty, sickness, stupidity, hate, TV, or anything you can sense or judge are not real unless you let them in to your "I am...." Similarly, wealth, health, intelligence, love, are not real unless you let them into your "I am...." The external world around you is only real to the extent your "I am..." will allow the real world into itself.

We are born with a natural, joyful, "I am..." soul being as part of the Infinite "I am...." This joyful soul contains love and is shared with all other "I am..." people and the Infinite. This "I am..." willfully grows and experiences more and more and more, with no limits, except for those simple limits that the "I am..." puts up, like no bad things, only goodness. Yes, the limits are created by ourselves and eventually are accepted by ourselves. Once "you are..." limits dominate, people imprison their natural "I am..." and it can be very difficult to see your joyful "I am..." and future experidigms. Everything is limited and imprisoned in whatever "you are..." block you have accepted. Yes, there are many bad people with imprisoned "I am...," but that does not mean you let them influence or impact your "I am...." Keep them away from your "I am...."

The "I am..." Infinite can be brought back to create your "I am..." with the !snap! of your fingers. In the instant you snap your fingers, you can awake to the Infinite and the joy of creating your "I am..." with experidigms. The Infinite "I am..." is always inside you no matter how bad the "you are..." is. Once again, you awaken the Infinite "I am..." in you, and you must engage it in your experidigm immediately before you are again challenged by the "you are..." of the external world. You have to use your experidigm muscle to keep it in shape and useful. You must know your own joyful "I am..." and keep playing for the higher and higher while you reject any "you are..." being thrust on and at you. It is always important to say "I am..." to a "you are...," because "No! I am not a ...." is just not good enough response to them. A "No!" carries an implied affirmation and subconscious acceptance of the 'you are...' statement. Your mind does not really hear "No!," but does hear and let in what comes after the "No!." So, saying "No! I am not a ..." repeating what the "you are..." said is dangerous for you as you let in to your mind what they say. Follow your "I am..." experidigm.

The Infinite "I am..." of all and love always exist in and around us, and are always ready to be brought into consciousness as "I am..." with all the benefits of future joyous experidigms. You picture your loving, joyous experidigm and connect with those who would love to participate with you in your experidigm choosing.

Of course, we can love as a team and truly be connected within an experidigm. As "you are..." you can love, but you are not really you and only temporarily connected and experiencing joy. Snap you fingers, and be "I am..." again. Snap your fingers and go to NEXT in the infinite line waiting for you to visualize and choose what fits your picture. There is always an infinite line of NEXT joyfully waiting for you.

We are given these human space suits to experience and explore "I am..." in a human form. This does not make anything physical real, except our "I am...." Our greatest joy is to experience choosing "I am...:" experiencing it, exploring it, and reaching to more and more levels. "You are..." means nothing and does not exist, unless your "I am..." makes it so. Only "I am..." exists, not "you are...," not the senses, not reality, not science – only the joy of "I am...."

PART 1:
Consciousness Context

The Beginning of "I am..."

"As a baby, life starts as a clean slate." I started *Choose Up* with this sentence and talked about the main choice each of us has in life, and that is to choose learning and experiencing. As a result, we live life joyfully. Choose to live life joyfully. As I wrote in *Turd Throwers Beware*, we live life joyfully if we learn to deflect the hurtful "you are..." redefining statements constantly bombarding us and reframing who we are. If we are not successful in deflecting 'you are...' bombardment, we lose our identity and become the version of the "you are..." being spouted at us. We can lose our "I am..." in all the "you are..." distractions of the world. Without our unique "I am...," we are lost in a joyless world. Our individual, unique "I am..." is always evolving with our "I am..." connection with the Infinite and with our connection to other "I am..." people. Realize the "I am..." already is connected to all and has access to all, and through accepting and acknowledging our "I am…" we have all and can be all.

This is very serious. DO NOT LOSE YOUR 'I am…!" I restate my original premise above: "As a baby, life starts as a clean slate, armed with our own "I am...." Our "I am..." is our unique, perfect connection to the Infinite, and this 'I am...' is the Infinite residing within us, as part of us, as one with us. We have access to the Infinite through our "I am..." oneness and uniqueness. Many religions would call this infinite by the noun God. Given we live in a "you are..." world of defining things for our own purposes, and defining things many times ends up giving human feelings to our "you are..." definitions and beliefs, the noun god has been "You are...d" to be in danger of losing "all... ness." God has been defined in human "you are..." terms and put in a box. To avoid all the "you are..." associated with society's use of god, I refer to the Infinite, and refrain from using "you are..." with the all Infinite, and just leave this at "Infinite" being all inclusion of good and god.

"I am..." is always within us and never leaves us because it is us. Unfortunately, "I am..." can be buried under so much 'you are...' as to be unrecognizable and appear to be lost. Sadly, an individual may not even know they have an "I am..." because a "you are..." controlled them before they understood and/or knew how to protect their "I am..." from a "you are...." Even sadder, is that an entire society can be under a "you are..." delusion; any "I am..." in such a "you are..." society is constantly under TTer and Taker attack. Knowing you have an "I am..." and nurturing it while under constant "you are..." attack is a struggle everyone has in life. Many lose the battle. This is not new to societal religions.

Many religions have an account of "you are..." overcoming the "I am..." connection in our minds, and then this overcoming becoming the reality in the world. The account of Adam and Eve[1] can be viewed in this way. A "you are..." serpent appears to Eve and puts "you are..." thoughts in her mind to challenge her "I am..." connection with the Infinite, and, sure enough, she disconnects her "I am..." and does what the "you are..." says, and buries her "I am..." connection. Then, Eve shares her new found "you are..." mistake with Adam, and the "you are..." keeps prospering in human history and keeps taking. I will put this in capital letters again: DO NOT LOSE YOUR "I am...." Yet, in any given day, there are trillions of "you are..." statements being spewed out of the mouths of UNconnected people trying to TAKE from the "I am..." (see *Avoid Takers* book to see how this is done).

This looks like a really big challenge to overcome "You are...," but thanks to the Infinite, which always exists in complete infiniteness everywhere and within us, nothing is more powerful than the "I am..." connection.

As the Infinite would have it, the "I am..." connection can be restored in an instant, anytime, anywhere. The most important act in any individual life is to enable your "I am..." and realize you are connected to the Infinite, and from that all joy flows as you experience and get connected. The freedom from "you are...," and recognition of "I am..." sets your temporary body space suit in motion to experience the choices you select from the Infinite. In your 'I am..." freedom, act with respect for life and love in your heart for all life, including yourself. Joy will follow you. We discuss in Chapter 2 how Joy works with the Joy equation.

Always be careful of the delusions of a judgmental "you are..." world trying to define you in their terms and take parts of your "I am..." and imprison the parts within your now delusional will. My earliest recollection of this is my first grade music teacher telling me "You are too loud for this choir, so you will only mouth the words of the song. You will not speak. You do not have talent." Unfortunately, no one had taught me at this time how to deflect "you are..." people and keep my 'I am..." fully operational. Today, 55 years later, I cannot read music, play music or sing. Every time I try, the "you are..." punches my "I am..." and says "shut up." This may seem trivial, but after being bombarded by millions of "you are..." statements for more than half a century, my inner "I am..." still functions freely and willfully connects with the Infinite and other "I am..." people every day. This book is the story of how the Infinite creates joy every day and how any "I am…" can be part of that joy.

"You are..." World of Delusions

I have been "officially" measured by so many different employment personality tests that I officially have a "you are..." designation to be controlled by and with. My Myers Briggs[2] (a standard personality test) personality classification is ENTJ or sometimes ENTS, or sometimes INTS, and it changes to others at times. I have many different four letter classifications to be controlled by. There was a time "I believed" what I tested as because it is "statistically" significant, and I thought it was OK to act in a certain way because that is the way the test says I am. That is a delusion.

I will never forget this startup company wanted to have each of the two hundred plus employees take a personality test so that the results "could help us work better together if we really knew who each other were." The owners wanted each employee classified into one of four types: driver, analytic, emotional, and social. The results were made public with rules on how to work with each type. Soon, the "drivers" were declaring they were in charge because they were "drivers", while the analytics were "pissed off" that they were declared geeks and laughed at and ostracized. As you could guess, classifying people as "you are..." led to all out distrust of each other and fostered unhealthy rivalry. In hindsight, it seems funny that we think classifying people helps in any way. It really is a stupid thought. Since an experience like this has happened to me several times, I realize it is pervasive to want to classify people as the "you are..." the test shows, so the testers and their bosses can control and manipulate those that are defined.

The bottom line is that "I am..." does not want to accept "you are..." and hopefully deflects it. Unfortunately, our human condition is such that people strive to "you are..." everybody, and put everybody in boxes and then try to control them. That is the account of Adam and Eve. Some enlightened societies try to limit "you are..." by having slander and libel laws to prevent outright harmful lying, but these attempts are only as guide rails on the road. It is very hard to legislate morality. A society is best to manage this by having respect for life and love in the hearts of its citizens. The bottom line is, whenever you hear the words "you are...," you should be very careful. It is hard because societies artificially create "you are..." manipulative statements and indoctrinate others as if the "you are..." is real.

Take Maslow's "Hierarchy of Needs"[3] as the classic definition for the stages on how a person lives and progresses from living as a savage to an enlightened spirit. Since Maslow created his definitions, people have been putting themselves into what part of his hierarchy they think they fit into in the immediate moment, and then they aspire to go to higher levels. Delusionally, individuals and society are defined as progressing through an evolution from basic human needs and survival to a high point of spiritual needs and understanding. Those who use this delusional schema classify people and societies as being at some level in the "needs" pyramid. They say, "You are such and such…" This is simply a "you are…" delusion of someone looking at life and making "you are…" classifications. What does exist is that the "I am…" can simultaneously exist in any, and all, and the complete infinite number of any "you are…" classifications ever made (probably as many as the number of individuals who have been on this planet). The "I am…" fits in no classification and can be infinite. The "I am…," if free and connected, can visualize what it is and wants to be, and then be that. Classifications limit your "I am…" and are a delusion.

Free Will Operates between "I am…" and "you are…"

I bet you are asking, "Is this "you are…" a different entity from my "I am…?" No, they are the same entity. They are different choices you make using your free will. When you make choices, you make them either using your connection to the creative Infinite with "I am…" or unconnected with "you are…" delusions. There is no duality. Your will chooses, and the real question is how much influence does your "I am… contribute, and how much does your "you are…" contribute. As 100% "I am…" you heal and create like Jesus, and as 100% "you are…" you define and murder like Adolf Hitler. We are born with free will searching to fulfill our "I am…" as we connect with the Infinite and many "I am…ers." That is how we start life, connected and joyful.

We have the gift of free will to make choices to be joyful in our "I am...."
And your choices belong to your "I am... and hopefully grow your "I am…
ness." Your "I am..." is connected to the Infinite "I am…" and all other "I
am…" people as you make choices to prepare your joyful experiences.
In my writings I view the infinite choices in front of us as a path toward
creativity and joy. The essence of "I am..." is creativity within the infinite
connective field of love, trust, and sharing. "I am..." drives our ability to
connect, create, love, and experience Joy.

Unfortunately, our "I am..." free will can be challenged by manipulative
and trained people who want to take our free will "I am..." for their own
self-serving purposes. They want to control your creative "I am..." free will
to use your creativity (which takers lack) and your "I am..." connections
for selfish purpose and their own enslavement in the Taker cycle problem.
These "you are..." dominate free will to attack the loving and susceptible
"I am..." free will and enslave that will. They attack "I am..." will using the
methods I describe in *Soaring to Awesome* and in *Avoid Takers*, with the
goal of 1) defining you the way they want to classify you and 2) taking your
"I am..." creativity for their own purpose. If an "I am..." will consciously
let these "you are..." attacks in, the "I am..." will choose the "you are..." and
reduce their 'I am...." connections. This is a dangerous point because just
how much "I am..." loss does it take to lose your "I am..." connection and
your creativity and become a Taker or TTer. In the extreme, the "you are..."
attacker and the "you are..." within join forces to reduce the "I am…" choice
to just a flickering light (But, "I am…" is never totally gone and can be
sparked back into dominance in your free will).

The "I am..." and "you are..." make up your free will choices, and you choose
in which mode you make your experience choices. Let me be clear—**operate in as much "I am..." as you can.**

There is no duality between "I am..." and "you are...." They exist in one free
will. They are the basic foundation of your free will to choose whether you
are connected or you are unconnected. Unfortunately, many may not know

that when they let "you are..." in, it will diminish "I am...," and will keep diminishing "I am..." until the "I am..." reaches a point of no longer being connected to the infinite connections. In some religions, this intentional disconnect is called "sin." Sometimes this disconnect is blamed on a spiritual third party (like the devil), but history shows it is a "you are..." TTer or Taker or your own will (subject to mass media delusion & hypnosis) that accepts the "you are..." definition and proposition and you become a disconnected Taker. It is easy to be a Taker -- no creativity involved, just manipulation and taking from a loving and sharing free "I am..." will.

Here are a series of three picture sets to visually show the relationship between "I am…" and "you are…" using a heart symbol. Why use a heart symbol? The heart pumps oxygenated blood throughout the body to be used by all cells. The "I am…" flows through all our cells if we let the "I am…" flow and deflect TTers from stopping it. If we let "I am…" flow we create "I am…" experidigms.

In the first set, pictures taken from the book *Soaring to Awesome -- Turd Throwers Beware* are shown as the back of the TTing protection shield seen on pages 175 and 178. The book talks about how attacks from a "you are…" can turn an "I am…" into a "you are…" blocked heart with little "I am…" flowing, if any. The first picture is a perfect unblocked heart that is unaffected by "you are…" and operates as an "I am…." Notice that life flows through the entire heart and the experidigm of life is "oxygenated" and enhanced by the four chambers: First, the filters of the "I am…" deflect "You are…;" Second, positive tools help visualize a new experidigm; Third, learning space allows experts and life to contribute; and Fourth, practice in various living contexts evolves the experidigm. Each chamber of the heart contributes to the "I am…" experidigm development, growth, and protection. The point of this heart analogy is to show that an individual allows life in to the "I am…" to experience the best "I am…" life. Having the best possible "I am…" life occurs only if one is free from "you are…" hurt and able to use tools, learn, and practice. The heart symbolizes the "I am…" acting in love.

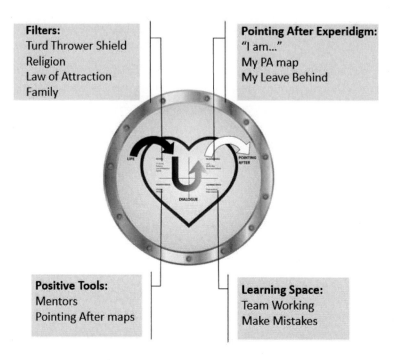

Filters:
Turd Thrower Shield
Religion
Law of Attraction
Family

Pointing After Experidigm:
"I am…"
My PA map
My Leave Behind

Positive Tools:
Mentors
Pointing After maps

Learning Space:
Team Working
Make Mistakes

The detail "I am…" heart is above and the same heart simplified is below. In the simplification notice the line at the bottom of the heart. Above the line is the functioning "I am… and below the line is the small "you are…."

The next two heart pictures are the detail picture and the simple picture of the "you are…" blocked heart. Unlike the open "I am…" heart, the blocked heart is almost fully by-passed because the 'you are…" took control of the "I am…" and does not let life and the blood flow to be fully oxygenated (or no filters, no tools, no learning, and no practice). The "you are…" only allows enough life flow and creativity to allow the "I am…" to create for them. The "I am…" is in danger of becoming enslaved by the external "you are…." The enslaved "I am…" heart is unconnected and unable to have meaningful experidigms until breaking free from "you are…."

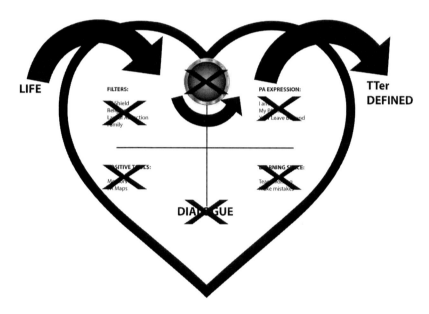

The detail "you are…" heart is above and the same heart simplified is below. In the simplification notice the line at the top of the heart. Above the line is the very small remaining "I am… and below the line is the dominant "you are…."

We will use the two simple pictures in the next two picture sets. I break each simple heart into its percentage "I am…" free will and "you are…" enslavement.

In this second picture below, we see the Infinite "I am…" as the all-encompassing area separating the connected "I am…" from the unconnected "you are…." Use free will and the TTer defection shield, this Infinite "I am…" is beyond the reach of the unconnected "you are…" reclassifying and renaming "I am…s." This Infinite "I am…" is always omniscient, omnipresent, omnipotent, immutable, and interconnected with all only good attributes like love, trust, mercy, grace, goodness, and joy. In this "I am…" connection, creative sharing and joy growth occur -- this is an eternal gift. In this area, we see connected "I am…" hearts that are 100% connected floating freely in the area. The "I am…" people are connected together and connected within the Infinite "I am…." On the boundaries of the area can be hearts with the "I am…" portion of heart in the area, but the "you are…" portion outside the area. The largely "you are…" hearts are 100% outside the area.

In this third picture below, a "you are..." Taker can entrap the "I am..." of an unsuspecting "I am..." or a willful "I am..." can convert to a "you are...." How this entrapment grows and grows until certain "I am...s" are no longer "I am...s" and are pulled into the "you are..." unconnected realm. This picture shows a fishing pole analogy where a "you are..." catches an "I am..." and plays them and controls them for "you are..." needs. A "you are..." will take from as many "I am...s" as they can. Whether the "you are..." is an individual, or a marketing campaign, or "you are..." leaders at work, or members of society, the effect on the individual "I am..." is the same - loss of 'I am...ness" and the related connections and ability to experience experidigms. Takers can keep taking to the point of keeping the "I am..." barely in the creative Infinite "I am..." and thus have access to creativity and connection that the Taker cannot do themselves and must take from the enslavement. The Taker may loss control of the "I am...er" at any time if the "I am…" declares "I am…ness" and focuses on an "I am…" experi-digm. The best way to free an "I am…" is use the deflection shield (see book *Soaring to Awesome*) and maintain the integrity of the "I am…."

Remember, we use our free will "I am…" or "you are…" as we try and cre-ate and build our experiences in life. The Infinite "I am…" is creation and connectivity, and the "you are…"is taking and unconnected. As an "I am…" person, all experiences can be created from the infinite now and as you evolve, you can keep adding more experiences and more Joy (and holi-ness). A "you are…" replaced "I am…" will try to take future experiences from someone else as a willful act of harm and taking. Of course, an "I am…" can make the willful decision and choose to be a "you are…." The allure of taking and the delusion of being in control can be false justifica-tion to become an unconnected "you are…."

Let's be clear. There are an infinite number of choices and experiences and connections that "I am..." can use, create with, and evolve while using the love and sharing of all "I am..." people. The "I am…" creates the experience and judges it with their individual "I am…" heart to see if the joy was captured. Any "I am…" person can receive joy through the connected experience. Native peoples feel the same "I am…" experience joy when they connect with nature and the Infinite "I am…." Maybe native people have an easier time because they may have less "you are…" people trying to take their "I am…."

Delusion of Walled Living

Classifications inevitably lead to defining differences between classifications. This creates a duality which leads to judgment about classifications. This judgment duality creates good versus bad. Delusions built on delusions are still delusions. Unfortunately, when we accept this "you are..." delusional world, we begin to label things good and bad, and, of course, we create fear around the bad. We must protect and defend ourselves from this fear. So we create the delusional need to build walls to keep the bad out. We have been building walls since the first "you are..." statement was made.

Ok, here is a quick quiz: Name a wall that has stood throughout history and still keeps out the bad people? I am smiling, because I hear you blurt out, "The "Great Wall of China". Yes, it is still standing. It keeps out nothing. It will continue to keep out nothing. The only reality is that you have an 'I am…" and if you wall it in, you have just disconnected yourself from the connected infinite, and you are right back in Eden taking that fruit from Eve and losing your 'I am….' Yes, an entire society can have mass delusion and lose their "I am…," and build walls. Yes, an entire society can delusionally protect itself and delusionally create enemies and fight wars and kill millions, tens of millions, and billions of space suits containing "I am..." throughout time. This does not make it any more real. This just means that the space suits holding these "I am..." are destroyed. The collective "you are..." delusions destroy our space suits, but they never destroy an "I am...." "You are..." has no power over "I am...." The Infinite is the power of the "I am..." by being the "I am..." and sharing the Infinite "I am..." connection.

Our "you are...ness" creates the delusion for protection, for the need for walls, for the desire to hurt those classified as different. This "you are..." prevents us from attaining the joy of life and disconnects us from the infinite connections of the "I am...." In Part Two, let's talk about this Joy equation and what to focus upon to live a continuously joyful life.

We are either connected to the Infinite or unconnected. Building walls is unconnected.

Step Out of Your Life

I know what you are thinking. You want to say to me, "Mark, there are crazy people out there who will kill me". I will say to you that your thought is a reflection of the 'You are..." society that has created that thought. 'I am..." only wants joy and does not exist in the duality of good vs evil. Connected "I am..." does not know or can create evil. For the Infinite, only good exists. "you are..." makes bad - that is the story of Adam and Eve. "You are..." is unconnected and can do bad.

Just step out of your life for a few minutes. Let's divide a page into two columns, and put "You are "on the top left and "I am..." on the top right. What do you do because the "you are..." of society expects it – write this on the left side of the page: you go to school, you work, you have family, you go to sports events, your buy things, you have friends, and you have material things. Now, what do you do because of "I am..." and you tell others "I am..." and write this on the right side of the page - you made what, you created what, etc. To what extent are you living your connected "I am ..." life or your "you are..." life?

Do not be afraid by the results. Do not fear. We know fears are delusions created in our "you are..." world to manipulate us.

The really crazy thing is that it is really easy to live an "I am..." connected life. Joy comes from an "I am..." connected life. In an "I am…" connected life you create your experiences and the resulting Joy

"I am..." Creates

Instead of creating a classification world with delusional duality, create a world of joyful experiences. The operational word in this sentence is "create." There are a couple of things that the "I am..." is exceptionally talented at doing. One is creating. The "I am..." can create from the infinite of possibilities. If the "I am..." cannot create, then the "I am..." needs to do the second thing that it is exceptionally talented at, and that is connecting with the Infinite and other 'I am....s" So, the "I am..." connects and creates in the infinite playground created by the Infinite.

We create an "I am…" playground. The above picture uses the cloud and heart picture to show a playground sandbox in the picture of a puzzle. The puzzle sandbox of life allows us to build what we like from any of the components we select. We can go to different sandboxes (i.e. other "I am …" sandboxes) and play. Each sandbox is a different context with additional choices. Explore other "I am…" sandboxes and learn and use what makes sense to your "I am…."

The "I am…" in everyone has the ability to see and create the future experidigm. Although the "I am…" sees the experidigm perfectly in the minds' eye, the actual creation and manifestation is less than perfect. This is why many artists keep wanting to improve the picture, the song, or the dance. That is because the experidigm is not perfect and will always be creatively evolving, and most important, the human creation does not contain and have the "I am…" within it. Unlike Pygmalion[4], the marble lifeless statue of our creation does not come alive with an "I am…." Only the Infinite "I am…" can create with infinite "I am…" in the creation. Most importantly, the human creation process is the time when human "I am…s" can join together in the creation process and experience joy. Joy is participating in the creative experidigm being connected to other "I am…s". The process of moving toward the experidigm in the loving and caring flow is joy. And this joy can be experienced every time we connect with "I am…" and experidigm.

Being connected to the Infinite, this "I am…" is not the egoistic me serving itself. The egoistic me artificially lives in the unconnected "you are…" delusional world and is artificially made in what is left after an individual accepts the "you are…" world. As we discussed, the "you are…" world creates classifications to manipulate others, and the terms ego, id and super ego[5] are terms made up and only exist if you agree with the "you are…" world. The individual "I am…" exists no matter what you believe. The issue with the "I am…" is you must connect with it to be able to access the Infinite and share it.

Be careful of this "me" ego thing which helps the "you are..." put the "I am..." in a small cage and helps the "you are..." dominate your life. Me is judgmental and possessive, building walls to create a duality and differences, and in this delusion of fear become hurtful. They say misery loves company, so the "you are...'s of the world create a lot of me. A very real danger of me can be slippage into addiction and the loss of the "I am..." connection as temporarily it appears Joy grows, but then stagnates with addiction. The unconnected me can stagnate in the same joy of the same experience and want more of that, and more of that, and get lost in the stagnation, especially if the me is disconnected from the "I am." The "I am..." loves the connection and the joy of going to the NEXT Experidigm while being connected, avoiding stagnation or addiction. We discuss much more later on being stuck and addicted in the stagnate joy you have captured and experienced so far. Just know that "I am..." contains respect and reverence for all life, including one's own, while the me can be perverted to addiction.

What You Let In

Your free will decides what you let in to your space suit.

I bet you have been in situations where people have insulted you and hurt you. You begin to take this personally. That is the wrong step because you let it into your mind. When you fight those that insult you, you can give them power because they plant all the anger, frustration, and hurt in you, and you begin to accept it and acknowledge its existence by fighting back. You think you are saying "no!" to it, but your mind puts anger and hate into you so you could fight bad. Now the "you are..." has a foot hold in you and starts minimizing your "I am..."

A better way to respond is to show love and talk only in love and act only in love, staying connected to the Infinite "I am..." In this way your mind ignores the existence of the bad "you are..." and you only support the love.

You do not need to win a hurtful argument; you walk away with love in your heart. If you do not accept their "you are...," they have to decide to keep it or not, but watching your love response will have a good model for them to follow, to just throw away the "you are...."

If you feel anger, frustration, or hatred, you have let in "you are..." words. Complaining with anger and frustration about others is a symptom you have let the "you are..." bad in your heart. The more complaining and repeating of "you are..." you do, the more you are slipping from love, creativity and connectedness. Others who like the delusion and taking of the "you are..." may like to hear you complaining, and this further helps you slip away from connected "I am...." Whole societies and religions can slip into the judging "you are..." mode and bring people down so they can manipulate and take from those who let in "you are..." frustration.

I know many of you may be thinking, "These people can really physically hurt me." I must protect myself." You protect yourself by getting away ASAP if you feel threatened physically. You do not protect yourself by acting like them, and letting anger and hatred in your heart, destroying your "I am..." and "I am..." connections. Keep your "I am..." connection by deflecting the "you are..." and avoiding Takers. If they are physical, let the law of society take care of them. If your space suit gets harmed, it is only temporary, and your "I am…" can be forever. Keep your "I am..." growing and connected.

Hopefully the dangers of the "you are..." world are very apparent to you. As you explore and learn from life, only let in the joyful life that works with your "I am...." We talk in the next part about a simple joyful equation that illustrates how the "I am..." joy can grow through life. Always looking and creating is part of the joy of life. Being connected to other "I am…s" in love and to the Infinite gives you perspective and discernment over the delusional "you are..." and related me. Being connected helps you stay away from addictive, stagnate behavior and pushes you along your learning curves. Yes, learning curves are a real part of the natural laws we experience using our space suit nature. We talk later how this relates to Joy.

The bottom line is that "I am..." is creative (not taking) and connected in a joyful way. You are not thinking so much as thoughts are freely flowing to your "I am..." receptive mind.

Trying to prove the delusions of the "you are..." world is fraught with peril. You will hear "you are crazy" a lot. Just goes to prove the point – you will be classified and branded "you are..." in any attempt to understand the delusions. Just say "I am...." You know you are in the "you are..." world when you feel fear and hurt. Anyone or thing that creates fear, punishment, or hurt should be deflected and then you declare your "I am..." and freely go to your NEXT experience.

Here is the really crazy part. There is no ordinary life. Everyone lives an incredible, fabulous, miraculous, adventurous life, and it is uniquely their life, because the Infinite "I am..." is in all of us as the greatest gift. Let that gift glow and create what that gift wants to give you. As we see in the next part: **the goal in life is to experience and connect with as much joy as the Infinite shows you.** Always make choices that move your "I am..." joy forward. As we shall see, never give up your ability to choose your experiences and connections.

A major tragedy I am addressing here is that many people cannot tell another person what they want, where they are going, and/or who they are because they are disconnected from their "I am...." A similar and equal tragedy is that people may think they know, but instead, they are living the life inflicted on them by a "you are..." society. It appears to be a constant struggle to keep your "I am..." free from the fear and resultant protectionism of the "you are..." world. This struggle begins to disappear when you learn to accept your "I am...ness" and live in your joy exploration with love and respect. No reason to judge or classify yourself. No spiritual reason to follow any way, buy your own infinite way living your connected "I am...ness." In your 'I am...ness" you have the power of the Infinite and your thoughts can become reality, in joyful and healing ways for you and others with whom you connect.

Who am I? "I am…"

Go and fill in your "I am…" by experiencing and connecting. Keep reaching for the joy of the infinite in the experiences you build for your "I am…"in this space suit you now have. Each "I am…" and each space suit in this world is different, so each connection you make adds to your ability to choose the new components for your evolving 'I am…'. Cherish each connection and grow. Connections assist with making selections and choices for each experidigm. Selections and choice have nothing to do with materialism or selfishness when they are related to the experidigm in the Joy equation because they are moralistically shared in the "I am…" connections. Selfishness and materialism are problems associated with being disconnected and belonging to the Taker cycle.

When saying "I am…." using positive statements is most essential and focusing on the NEXT positive experidigm gives needed direction and connection with other supportive "I am…ers." Of course there will be bad days, when the "you are…s" of the world beat the individual "I am…" down, and when the TTers shield was not used to defect TTers. Some "you are…" might make its way into your "I am…." Some start feeling bad and mentally say awful and delusional negativity to their internal own "I am…:"

+ "I am depressed"

+ "I am stupid."

+ "I am evil"

+ "I am a loser"

+ "I am not…"

+ "I am worse than…"

+ or any negative I am… statement

Never ever be negative. This will drag one to become a "you are…" taker. Always point up to an experidigm and just go and experience it. Some feel as though they are trapped and have given up. No—point up to the experidigm and do. Most things will not happen as you want, but we have NEXT. People are not in control of change. People are in control of their experidigm and using positive NEXT to move forward.

Debate Challenges

Understanding and nurturing the "I am…" is the single largest challenge in life. Our attention must focus on how to evolve our "I am…" in a world that wants to define and classify our "I am…" and mold the "I am…" to what the status quo wants. The biggest delusion in life is to believe we can prevent change and create certainty within our society. Society tries to lock in certainty by fitting everything into a definition and keeping it there, trying to lock it into place. Once defined, anything that challenges the definition and wants to change, it is challenged and forcibly required to get back in the definition. Of course, this fitting into the definition and classification is a delusion. Almost all debates you will hear in a political and social forum are a struggle for the winner to define and classify he opponent in a "you are…" way. Why? The winner of a "you are…" debate gets to be in charge of the definitions of society and gets to take from that society on those definition terms. There are only three types of social debates:

1) "You are…" versus "you are…:"

The "you are…" versus "you are…" debate is the most common in society. Each side tries to define one's opponent as something "bad" and brands them as bad, and all of their "facts" are intended to show how bad the opponent is. For example, saying "you are a liar" focuses the discussion on one trait, lying, and whether this is proven or not, the opponent is branded as such, and the accuser hopes the opponent will lose because of this. Very little, if any discussion on how to reach an experidigm because this is not what a Taker is after. The Taker creates the problem for others to get others involved, and once involved, the vanquished are captured in the Taker cycle focused on the Taker's problem.

There is no winner in this debate because the end result is a definition of the world that only benefits the winning Taker.

2) "You are…" versus "I am…:"

Unlike the first debate, the participants in this example share their "I am…" and what they stand for and what their experidigm might look like if "I am…ers" want to connect and share. The only way the "you are…" wins the debate is if the "I am…" tries to discuss or deny the constant "you are…" statements against him or her. As the Turd Thrower shield shows, deflect "you are…" accusations by affirming your "I am…" statements, never addressing the "you are…" statements. Just ignore the "you are…" statements. The only way a "you are…" wins is if he or she successfully redefines the "I am…" as the "you are…" wants.

3) "I am…" versus "I am…:"

Interestingly, since the "I am...s" are already connected and sharing, the debate is a discussion of how to work together to handle the changes that are occurring all around them. The debate allows the clear position of each side to be articulated so that the debaters can find common ground to work on in the future, even though they may have significant differences. This type of debate is an ongoing discussion that keeps benefiting all parties.

If a "you are…" wins a debate, the tendency is to" pull up the rope" and lock in the definition of the problem that the "you are…" defined. With the rope up, any debate or dialogue stops and the status quo defends the definitions and focus on the Taker cycle problem. Clearly, this creates a delusion that the status quo and "you are…" can prevent change and lock in security with the definition and problem it maintains. However, change is certain and will overcome the status quo. History shows that many people may get hurt in the process of the 'you are…' status quo defending against change. Change will overturn any wall. Only an "I am…:" has the creativity to flow with change in joy.

Creativity Disclaimer

I should not really have to say this, but your experiences must be built on a moral foundation. The written moral foundation of the Ten Commandments is a good start. The golden rule of "loving your neighbor as yourself" is also included. Lastly, the Infinite only created and knows good (no evil), so only create good for your "I am…" and for everyone and everything else. The only evil you will encounter to challenge your "I am…" is a willful "you are…."

Please do not take this as a threat or as trying to instill fear in you as a "you are…" type of statement (i.e. like - you are a sinner)", but, THERE IS NOTHING WORSE THAN HAVING YOUR "I am…" DISCONNECTED FROM THE INFINITE AND FROM OTHER 'I AM…" CONNECTED PEOPLE. Each individual is willfully in charge of this connection. Please willfully opt in to your "I am…" connection and keep it evolving. Carpe Diem.

One's "I am…" is connected only to goodness. Our "I am…" expresses only goodness. When you express non-goodness, like "I am bad, I am evil…," this is the impact of your mind repeating the "you are…" hypnotism of the world. You must shake off the "you are…" hypnotic and delusional world and keep on expressing your connected and creative experiencing "I am…." If you feel bad, that is the "you are…" world you accidentally let in, and it covered over your "I am…." The only way to get back from a 'you are…" delusion is to get connected to the Infinite "I am…" and other "I am…ers" who experience joy. When your 'I am…" experience feels the joy of the Infinite, you are starting down the path of life toward more joy and connection. Keep experiencing joy.

PART 2:

Infinite Joy

Driving Life

Life is motion. If you are physically moving and flowing, you are physically alive. What are you flowing toward, choosing to think about, pointing at, and doing to keep flowing? Most important is, what is the end pointing after experidigm you are directing your effort toward? This directed effort defines your life at any point. Without a future experidigm aim, a car, or a plan, or anything that moves will eventually just run out of room and just stop, maybe lost. *Man's Search for Meaning* by Victor Frankl[6] implies that the pointing after experidigm aim is what gives life purpose and keeps one alive and moving.

Religions and philosophers have looked at what the purpose in life might be, and they note that everyone dies and is soon forgotten as to whom they really were. Some see no meaning at all in life on earth (i.e. *Ecclesiastes* in Old Testament[7]), so no need to "strive" for wealth, power, etc., except to live in the joy the Infinite bestows on you) Then, maybe the driving force in life is joy from the Infinite, shared through love and connections.

Live life with creating joy as your consistent purpose and goal. You create your joy as you create your experidigms. You do not know the details of your future, so explore the choices you have.

The Joy equation takes for granted that a society has a certain free and shared simple moral framework that all in society understand and live by on a daily basis. If members of society break the moral law, a system of moral training is required for them until they are able to live by the simple moral code. A simple moral code might be the Ten Commandments. The Joy equation is not naive in that it does contain allowance for hurtful TTing people who will take away individual and societal joy. Although they negatively impact joy, the TTers are not beyond the moral "law" and should be subject to avoidance and punishment by society. The hurtful TTers are allowed to participate with the discretion of the moralistic and connected "I am...." Unfortunately, not all societies are moral. In the case of dictatorships or strong militaristic leaders, the leaders act in their own self-interest and hurt anyone who is different. Even in dictatorship and military situations, the individual and small groups can operate within the Joy equation and their supportive internal morals, but doubtful the larger society will support any moralistic behavior beyond what the dictator allows.

At a similar extreme as a dictator, a moral society with hundreds of strict laws that hinder "I am...' connections is just as restrictive. The more judgments a society thrusts on its members, the less the society will connect with "I am..." and the more its members will fight change and keep the status quo. However, an individual could still focus on the Joy equation and have experidigms and connections, and thus receive some form of joy.

Individual Joy: What experidigm do you want written on your tombstone? "Shit Happens" is wrong -- your expectations happen, and if shit is your expectation, it happens. Look in the mirror -- your joy is based on you and no one else, except all those you share your joy with in a whole life. Create your joy experidigms and let the Infinite "I am..." see through your eyes, and make everything fresh and infinite in scope.

Let the Infinite see the joy you see. Be thankful for the joy each day. No fear, just joyful days.

Connected Joy: Expressed as freedom to experience your own Joy and experience with others theirs if you choose to do so. Experience common joy together with shared pointing after experidigms like sports, eating, music, working, etc. Know what each other is pointing at to receive. Let go, listen and all comes together. Each person drives his or her "I am…" life with other "I am…s."

Infinite Through Your Eyes

The Infinite is looking through one's eyes into the world. I have to make a choice. What do I want the Infinite to see? This sounds like a difficult choice: right or wrong? The pressure is on to get it right. At least that is what the judgmental part of one's brain keeps thinking.

Then I realize that this is not a test. This is not something on which I am being judged. It is really simple. Simple that I am either connected to the Infinite or not. Either the Infinite sees well through my eye and sense filters or not. "Or not" means that the Infinite no longer looks through my eyes, and I get disconnected. Once disconnected, I slip into the "you are…" Taker world.

I choose to "see well" and connect with those that "see well". I will play and do and work with a smile on my face and love in my heart, and see the world and my future from a positive perspective. My experience teaches me that when I am creative, using my creativity to learn, to build, to share, and to connect, I am the moist joyful. I want the Infinite to see through my eyes that joyful creative world with me. Together connected, all the knowledge ever and the laws of the universe are available for this creative joy. I choose smiling, love, creativity and sharing, and the joy of the Infinite flows through my eyes.

I said it was simple. Just look at your new positive experidigm with creativity and sharing and a smiling loving attitude. Your joy will start showing through, and you will gather/attract what your experidigm shows you and the Infinite, and with those with whom you share the "I am…" connection.

Now, life is very, very, very hard if I choose bad, looking at the world with envy, disdain, hatred or any other negative emotion that has me judging anyone or anything in the world. Do you think the Infinite wants to look through my eyes judging the world negatively? Frankly, judging seems like an attempt to play like I am a god-king; so really, does the Infinite want to connect and see through these judgmental eyes. Very doubtful. I know when I am angry, frustrated, and non-loving, I just see the world as bad and judge it as bad. Worst of all, bad thoughts dominate my thinking. In my negativity and judgment, I block out almost all "I am…" connections, and put 100% blockage in my life. Unfortunately, I sever the Infinite "I am…" connection. No joy flows, and the Infinite no longer looks through my eyes. I have to drop this negativity and judging and bring on my creativity to reconnect.

How do I reconnect to the Infinite and to joy? I do not go into meditation, nor do I disconnect from the world in anyway. I look for joy; I look for love; I look for flow of life, and realize that life flows. Life flows toward joy if not constrained by bad people. When I look at a scene in nature or in a big city, or anywhere life is flowing, I see that life is constantly interacting, changing and recreating every second. I am part of this recreating if I choose to be. If I choose, I reconnect, and I am in the life flow. We naturally know how to connect and share, to be part of the flow. The Infinite built the flow, is the flow, and invites you to be part of the flow.

It is so very important to know the Infinite sees through my senses. Do not expect the impersonal flow to give anything to you. Do not expect to get back joy, material wealth, love, or any other earthly type of emotion good or bad. It is just the impersonal flow. It is your ability to create that makes the joy for you, as you create for you and other "I am…s", the Infinite sees through your eyes, and smiles at your creations.

How fleeting is that joy? Do you have an open creative mind, or do you slip into the status quo or negative judgments -- you choose how fleeting your joy is by choosing to connect and create evolving experidigms. Just be creative and invite the Infinite creative to see through your eyes. Get past your fear created by organized religion that god is judging you and that only god is creative. You are creative in your "I am…ness". You are the Infinite "I am…s" child with access to all infinite choice, and the Infinite 'I am…" is always in you. The Infinite has already created all choice from which you can select. Your fears of the unknown, of change, of criticism, of anything, block the connection with the Infinite to see through your eyes and thus limit you. Fear keeps you in the artificial status quo, as the creative world flows on without you. It might feel good to be "happy" with your station in the status quo, but this is false and transitory and based on external influences, 100% percent out of your control or influence. You control 100% internally only. The external "happy" cannot be maintained and leads to ups and downs and searching for the "middle way" to be happy. The middle way is just another state of fear that keeps you comfortable right where you are, both physically and mentally. When you stay where you are, others are evolving internally visualizing and doing their infinite experidigms. Break from your 'happy comfort" fear and be connected with the Infinite in you. Use your internal creativity to joyfully flow with change in the world around you.

Another fear is that other unconnected "you are…" people may or will try to hurt you. Ok, they will try to hurt you and take from you. The only way they can create is through you, as your "I am…" is connected. They temporarily connect through you and take that from you, but only if you allow them. They will try whether you are hiding from them or whether you declare your creative experidigms. You must focus on your "I am…" connectedness, your pointing experidigm, and deflect and avoid those that try to stop you and take your connectedness.

I know that overcoming fear might appear difficult, but it is like overcoming your initial fear of driving. Once accomplished, you drive every day. While driving a car, you have your eyes open, your mind focused on the road ahead of you and where you are going. If you get lost, you ask for help and get back on track with the help of others. You are focused on what's in front of you and the vision of where you are going. You do not fear where you are going. You are not focused on what is behind you, what is happening in some foreign country, or the claims of media. If you lose focus, you risk getting in an accident that may hurt you slightly or may even kill you. Taking your eyes off the road ahead of you is very bad.

This driving example is very similar to visualizing your experidigm and journeying towards it. You focus on where you are going, and you tell friends where you are going so they can either 1) take care of your things/place while you are gone, or 2) know where you are going to help or comfort you. If you have any issues on your trip, you connect with your friends or get the opinion of experts (i.e. car mechanic to fix broken car). If you lose focus and get lost and do not seek friends or experts, you may get unconnected until you decide to be connected again.

If you are driving, and instead of looking down the road, you start text messaging, you lose focus and can have a serious accident. You have willfully chosen to disconnect from your flow. The cell phone is a symbol for TTers or Takers who will distract you from your experidigm. To receive your joy, stay focused and connect with others on your experidigm.

The Infinite is looking through your eyes into the world. You and the Infinite smile at the same time as you focus on and do your experidigm.

Know that joy and happiness are different. With joy, "I am…" and joy are one and connected with the evolving experidigm – we coexist together fully. Happiness is fleeting and only exists outside you and outside the experience. Joy lasts and continues as we continue on to an evolving experidigm. It is like being in a general retail store with everything, although at this moment you only select a few items. All the others items still exist and are available to enhance your joy later as you move to your NEXT experidigm. You are in the full joy of the general store. That is the full joy of living in your experidigm. An infinite number of selections is always around you, and you live in that joy.

Equation of Joy

Like Solomon says in the Old Testament book, *Ecclesiastes8*, life and all the actions in life are meaningless; instead, the infinite wants to grant us joy. Accomplishments, success, and judgments have no meaning in the big picture or small picture of life. What is left is the flow of "I am…" joy in life, the ability to connect in love and keep moving joy along and upward. Joy flows from the Infinite to us and we have access to all the joy (in the proverbial general store) in infinite ways.

Joy is not static. Joy is actively captured through the flow of our experidigm experiences. Joy is related to the number and types of experiences (experidigms) we have. Joy is also directly related to the number of meaningful "I am…" connections we have. Unfortunately, less joy is directly related to the number of TTers and Takers we experience and do not deflect. The most simplified straight forward equation for joy is expressed as:

Joy = (Σ experidigms) X (# connections) - ΣTTers

In words, the sum of all experidigms times the sum of all connections minus the sum of all turd throwers and takers results in a joy number. What is most important is that the joy number is positive and moving more positive over time to avoid stagnation. The magnitude of the number has no meaning. This simple equation helps illustrate how to stay in positive, non-stagnant joy. The more experidigms we have, and the more connections we have naturally create more joy -- more possibilities to experience something new and joyful. However, the amount of joy is limited by the sum of the number of TTers and Takers we have trying to stop us. In fact, if we have only one connection and one experidigm, and we have 2 TTers, we have negative Joy (1x1-2=-1). For many people, this is what family life is like with both parents as TTers and being young school age with only one experidigm and very limited connections. Home life is no joy. If the children's educational life is filled with even more TTing bullies, then they see no joy in school as well, with the negative school joy number as high as the number of TTers. Instead of feeling stuck in this situation, it is extremely important to devise an individual's own experidigms and make connections with those other "I am..." connections who have infinite connections and share and contribute to enhance the individual's experidigms.

The Joy equation shows that there are three things to do to always raise and move joy positively (it assumes you are always connected to the Infinite within you):

1) Get more connections who are connected. You will see so many more points of view and different life contexts to illustrate how the world is bigger than where you are at now.

2) Create new experidigms to explore. Do and learn from and share these experidigms with your connections.

3) Avoid Takers and deflect TTers so that you have no one entering your "I am..." who you do not want there.

Let's play with how someone can grow with this equation through life. When we are born, we have one experidigm (our original "I am...ness") and our only connections are our parents, which we hope are "I am..." connected and not TTing Takers. As a baby in this example, we have positive joy (1x2-0=2). That is good. Each day the baby and young child gain more experiences and grow in their "I am...ness." It may stay like this until the child goes to school, where he or she can make many more connections and see new experidigms for the first time outside the core family. If the youngster joins a team, like sports or reading, and has positive connections, then joy is rapidly increased with many more connections and positive experiences. The joy score goes into double digits (actually, there are no limits to the Joy score). But if the child joins a team, and teammates become TTers, the youngster can fall in a deep negative hole, as the TTers recruit other TTers to harass the target youngster.

We do not choose to be in a deep negative joy hole; others put us there with the "you are..." TTing. We could have helped ourselves out of the hole by asserting our "I am..." and deflecting TTers and avoiding Takers, AND, by making other connections that have a relationship to the experidigms we were visualizing and acting toward attaining. The "you are..." hole created by TTers and Takers can be deflected away from you and fully disappear.

A hole caused by no or very few experidigms can be filled in and eliminated by connecting with other connected people and groups who encourage dialogue in their groups, so that "I am..." can visualize what might be NEXT. Here is what sharing an experidigm looks like:

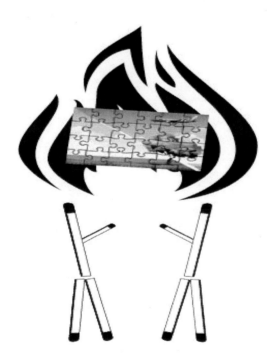

The picture shows the experidigm being shared in all the fullness that can be visualized. Then as shown below, the individual "I am..." picks their choices in specific areas with the assistance of the connected group.

The hole is hard to get out of if we do not visualize an experidigm and connect with those who can add to it. The thing about experidigms is they attract connections who are interested in them, and when experidigms attract TTers, just deflect them away. Use the deflection shields described in *Soaring to Awesome – Turd Throwers Beware*.

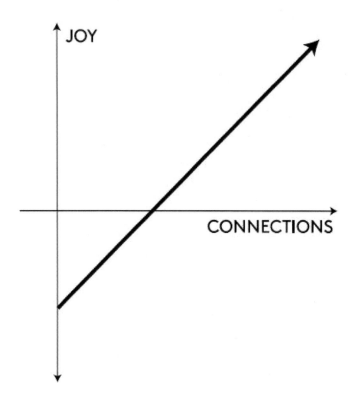

The above graphic shows a situation where the number of experidigms and TTers is kept constant as the number of connections to support the experidigm is increased. If one has 1 experidigm, and 3 TTers, then for each connection added one gets to offset 1 TTer. Having three total connections will offset all three TTers, so adding more connections past that will bring the Joy equation into more and more positive. This is a simple situation holding experidigms and TTers constant. The reality is life allows the number of experidigms, the number of connections, and the number of TTers to change on a daily basis. To have positive joy in life we must increase the number of experidigms and connections while deflecting TTers and avoiding Takers.

If a person now creates two additional experidigms to have a total of three experidigms, with the three connections and the three TTers, the resultant joy is now positive six. In a world where many individual TTers and TTers groups exist, joy is only accomplished by creating more experidigms and more connections. The equation says it is important to learn to eliminate the TTers in ones' life. If the number of TTers is kept at bay, then one can have many experidigms with work, family, school, play, friends, hobbies, music, doing, sports, church, and so on. With each experidigm type, many connections types can be added.

When we are young, we are sometimes limited in making more and better connections because we have a limited view of the world. Young people tend to connect with those at home and at early school. Further, young people are just beginning to understand how to create experidigms and slowly make just a couple of experidigms. The equation shows how susceptible the young are to one day having positive joy and one day having negative joy when a group of TTers harasses them. This oscillating joy occurs if the child has no exposure to or training in deflecting TTers and using the TTer shield. If a person gets isolated into one experidigm with few connections, it only takes a few TTers to create negative Joy.

It is imperative at a very young age to learn this equation and develop creative skills to attract new experidigms and to attract those connections who can assist you in moving forward while asserting your "I am..." to all the "you are" TTers.

As we gain more experience by playing sports, by practicing arts (drawing, writing, music, etc.), by learning school subjects, by traveling, by cooking and eating, by working (volunteer and pay), and by many other activities, we gain exposure to more possible experidigms and their related connections. We can have many experidigms at an early age by trying the many different ideas to which we are exposed. It is within the individuals control how to get ideas from books, from experts (teachers), from history, from relatives, from professionals, and such, as we can spend our time, energy and money (what little we have), learning about other experidigms. The example biographies in the Appendix share that reading books was a strong source for creating new experidigms and the associated joyful transitions. Being a doctor or lawyer are just a couple of ideas among millions of other career options.

As people mature, people talk about building a career. Whatever a career is, it is still bounded by the Joy equation. Within your career, it is best to seek out new opportunities (i.e. experidigms) and build your number of connections, while deflecting TTers (and you are great at this as you get older). If you limit your number of connections and experidigms to your current boss, you are on very shaky joy ground (like being a new born baby totally dependent on your parents being connected and not being subject to TTers). If you lose your boss and at the same time lose your connections and your only experidigm, you are stuck at work with zero work joy. You need more "I am…" help if you have not prepared to deflect TTers. If you have TTers, you are in negative joy, and that is awful.

At work, individuals can build their own experidigms, even in the context of the overall company and functional department experidigms. Please read the first several chapters of *Soaring to Awesome* to see how many experidigms can exist in business and how to manage the business status quos that may exist. Individual work experidigm futures can include: learning future, skills future, leadership future, product-making future, functional-position future, and team future. The individual experidigm can be one of these or all of these and change over time. Important in all cases is to share the experidigm and adjust from feedback as necessary. For example, an experidigm might be to be a leader on a project team for a new product and learn leadership skills and an understanding of the product. Next, might be a program leader of many projects, setting the context for each project.

When a person becomes a member of an existing group with an existing experidigm, and the number of TTers is kept very low, the resultant joy will be positive and significant. For example, one new experi‹ ͓ one hundred new connections minus five TTers is a very positive 95. On the surface that looks good. Yet, groups can have serious issues. The group status quo wants to ensure static norms in the group, and when the group judges that a member challenges the group norm, a majority of the group could possibly turn into TTers to the individual. In this example, if all one hundred group connections turn into TTers, the resultant joy number would be minus 104. That is a large shift. This is more common than one would think. In groups that may be judgmental, like politics and religions, quick judgements can lead to immediate public outcry against an individual. The Joy equation shows it is not best to but "all your experience eggs in one basket." Have many levels of experidigms in different subject matters and other groups with their own connections.

As an individual progresses through life, the trend would be to keep adding both more experidigms and more connections while becoming an expert at deflecting TTers. This would allow the individual to keeping moving joy forward and sidestepping both negative stagnation and addiction. Unfortunately, how to create experidigms (big picture thinking) and how to find connections is rarely addressed in modern educational systems. I discuss how this can be added to educational systems by year of study in Part 7.

You may ask, is this equation applicable universally and uniformly across all societies, all cultures, or is it specific to "industrialized" cultures? Certainly, the equation applies to cultures that have the ability to "connect" and to have experiences, which are both part of industrialized cultures. A native culture, defined as living solely off the land with no electricity, aggregates into a group of people. This group of people communicates with each other and works together at times for a common good, like making food and eating. If they communicate, they can connect to work together on a common vision, like eating good food. Although it looks like they have limited choices to make experiences, this might be deceiving. Maybe they have more choices than appears, more selections from the nature they know so well around them. They can choose to hunt one day and choose to run or swim another day. A native society has the ability to visualize experiences and choose which experience they want, and to share this experience with other connections for them to add to or subtract from. All cultures and societies have the ability to experience and connect.

Another way to see the Joy equation is to use visuals for each component of the equation as shown below. Joy is about sharing and reaching the experidigm, so the joy picture shows sharing of a reached experidigm. The experidigms step picture shows the relationship of puzzle experidigms as steps to the NEXT experidigm, and there is not just one staircase, but many staircases for each portion of life, whether it be work, family, social, or play. The picture for connections shows how the experidigmer points to the experidigm and manages the inputs from those connected to the experidigmer to improve the experidigm. The TTer illustration shows the shield which lists the six types of turd throwers. Keep adding puzzle experidigm steps and connections to attract joy.

Visual Joy Equation

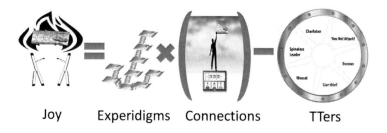

Joy   Experidigms   Connections   TTers

Let's take this equation to the extreme. In history, there are times when conquering armies take away any physical freedom from their captives. The victors enslave the vanquished in camps and force them to perform awful physical and mental tasks, even torture and many times ending in death. The Holocaust during World War II is a clear example. In this situation, with the Joy equation, the ΣTTers is very high, and Σexperidigms is very low approaching zero. One would expect the Joy equation to have a very negative score, even if the vanquished prisoners had sympathetic connections with others. Faced with this negative score, many lose hope. In this hopeless feeling their Σ experidigms goes to zero and they stay in negative joy where the sum of the ΣTTers becomes overwhelming. Sadly, giving up can lead to death. But, humans are different than other animals and do not have to give up. We can imagine and create in our minds, no matter how bad the external world is. We can imagine and visualize internal experidigms that are so wonderful, that any external world is meaningless. If we can keep our physical space suit body functioning, we can live in our own internal joy. In the internal world of the mind, the ΣTTers can be internally deflected to zero and what exists is a beautiful Σ experidigms the mind creates. Those who survived the horrors of the World War II camps talk of their mental Σ experidigms, such as returning home and living in love with their families.

How can we get stuck in negative joy? This can be where the person is stagnant in the same experidigm (creating something like a prison) and adds few connections, never enough to overcome the number of TTers. Below is a sample graph of never overcoming TTers.

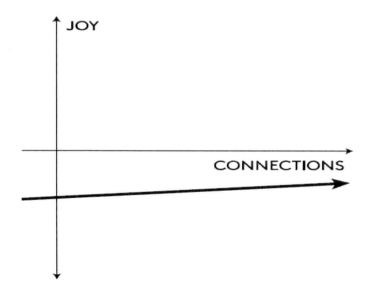

Our human minds are connected to the Infinite, thus we have the ability to choose the Joy equation and accept our joy at any time we choose. It is our willful choice. The Σexperidigms we create give us freshness in our joy, our connections give us strength of options, but ΣTTers distract us. We need to deflect them, just as we deflect bad situations. We have urgency to keep our joy fresh to ignore and avoid bad situations from staying in our minds.

Additive Joy Equations

The simple Joy equation can be additive when a group of "I am…" people forms together in a community. All the Joy equations come together with all the joy being combined. It is wonderful to increase all the surrounding joy and impact everyone positively. In a perfect world, all the positive connections and experidigms make for even greater cumulative joy beyond what an individual may achieve.

Be careful. If all members have similar connections and experidigms, but different TTing Takers, then the group might bring in more negative TTers than positive connections and experidigms resulting in negative joy. Always pay attention to how others are handling their TTers and how many they have that are active and hurtful. Even within a group, live within your "I am…" and not a "you are…." The previous graph shows that the Joy equation never becomes positive when many TTers dominate the equation. As more individual connections are added, more hateful TTers groups are added. As more experidigms are attempted, more TTers from the status quo try to stop the change. Limit the number of TTers that other groups bring to your additive Joy equations. Obviously, controlling the impact of TTers is key to experiencing joy. If one has no TTers, one has a high probability of a positive upward joy line. Know that because joy is shown publicly, TTers will attempt to take that joy.

Step Function Joy Equation

The simple linear equation could instead be a step function because we want to stay at certain joy levels until we have enough connections to try new or more experidigms. Until we get enough connections to help us, we might just stay where we are, and we do not "employ" the new connections until we head to the NEXT experidigm. All these new connections suddenly appear all at once in our Joy equation and our joy leaps to the next level. This experidigm infrastructure building from which we can experience more experidigms is important to building more complex and complete experidigms.

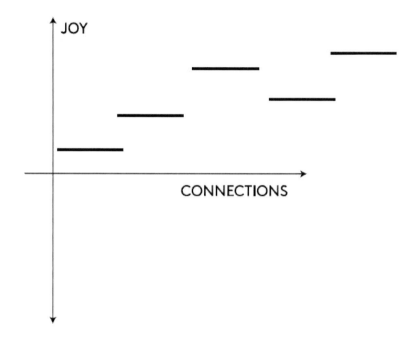

Imagine that a step function is like a stair case reaching higher and higher (as shown on the cover of *Choosing Up* and here).

After each step is a small landing to ensure finalization of that of that step and to prepare for the next experidigm step. Each step has elements of a physical, spiritual and connected experidigm. The higher the steps go, the greater the scale and scope. As the steps go higher, the supportive infra-structure of love, trust, care, choice ability, and access to doing, all grow as the infrastructure and experience grow.

Each new experidigm builds on the backstory of each previous step. The backstory is the flowing wave upward of joy and love that propels the "I am…" to grow and connect with other "I am…s." Your choices are your "I am…ness" in the context of your experidigm. Notice the graph shows a step change dip down when TTers are successful in making your NEXT experidigm fail. Deflect them and do a NEXT experidigm and the step change goes up. Never give in to TTers.

Building a strong infrastructure of connections and previous experidigms is a good thing. Individual have their steps, yet these steps fit into a bigger picture of the group.

Another way to visualize the step function is to see different NEXT choice balls on levels of the spiral opening upward toward infinity. A step is one of the rungs of the opening up spiral and it is connected with other waves, and at the connection of the waves.

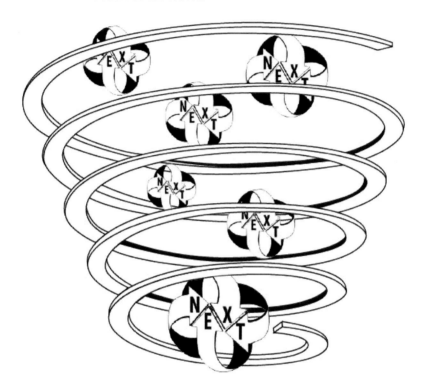

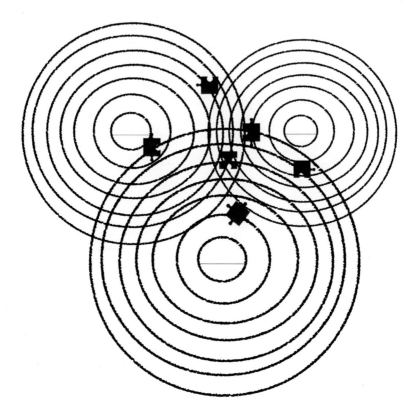

Role of S-Curves

The role of an S-curve here in this context is to show the impact of change through time. The x-axis is no longer connections, but time, and the y-axis is still Joy. All experidigm changes start slow, and then have a period of rapid growth. Then they slow down again and continue on rising slowly at a higher level as shown below.

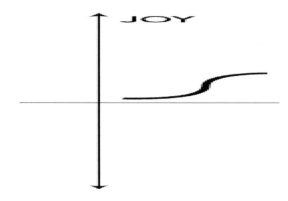

This type of S-curve is a fact of nature when it comes to showing how much of the population has experienced the full change. Joy may be like this over time. We can experience it all at once, or much more probable is that we experience an S–curve over time as we experience the "I am…" experidigm. When we have a new experidigm, we feel a slight increase in Joy (from the experidigm and new connections), and as our experidigm grows, it may expand rapidly by attracting many more connections (and associated new potential experidigms). Thus, our Joy may grow rapidly. When the number of connections slows, our joy will slow down and remain consistent at that level.

When the Joy slows, we should already have new experidigms in the works that are allowing our joy to grow. In this way, we are always growing our Joy with new and higher S-curves one after another or combined together. Since the Infinite gives us infinite choices, we have an infinite number of S-curves from which to choose.

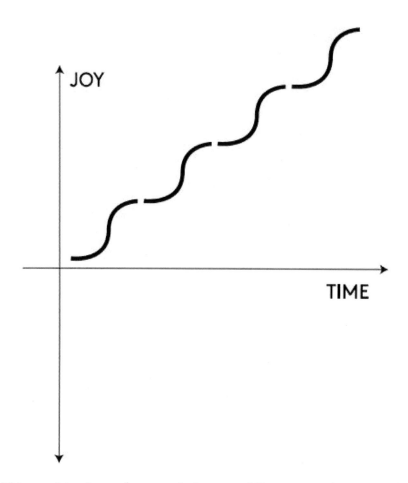

This graphic above shows each S–curve following another experidigm S–curve.

What changes on these S-curves is the length of time we spend in each of the three phases of the curve (i.e. the slow startup phase, the fast experience growth phase, or the slow stagnation at the end). The fast expansion growth phase is exhilarating. Sometimes the slowing phase is a welcome break, but the NEXT experidigm should already be planned and in progress. We must be careful not to rest on our laurels and get too complacent with where we are with joy. Being mired anywhere on the S-curve is the same – being stuck. We must learn that creating a new experidigm can always unstick us.

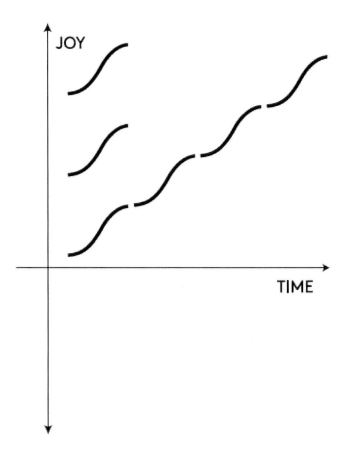

The S-curves do not have to be in sequence following each other. A better way is to have several experidigms happening at the same time in different areas of our life: like work, sports, music etc. Manage them as life and focus permits. The reality is we have a complete composite of experidigms that we can decompose and focus on that which needs focus. Any given experidigm can be put into a parking lot to do later when more appropriate, but it still exists -- in this case the initial slow phase will be much slower.

All these types of equations probably feel somewhat artificial and surreal. Of course they are unreal. Like all equations, they are just a simple approximation of joy in life and what we should focus on and when. They help us focus beyond our distractions and the challenges of life, and deflect TTers. We can focus on increasing the number of experidigms and "I am…" connections in our life and this will help our joy. We are in charge of willfully choosing "I am…" from all the infinite possibilities in front of us. Let's talk a little about choosing.

Choice Symbols:

The arrow symbol on the cover of this book shows how we ask NEXT from the Infinite and choices come to us. The choices can be experidigms or the component choices within each experidigm, or the connected people for each experidigm.

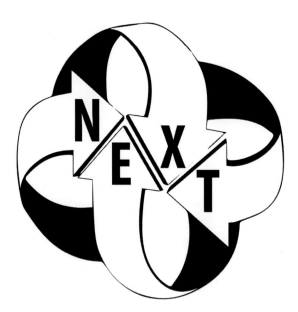

As this symbol shows, there will always be choices to enable another NEXT to keep increasing our joy. If the NEXT does not increase our joy, we just get another NEXT, and we keep getting another NEXT to keep getting more joy.

Problems occur when we either stop asking for NEXT or get stuck or we are unable to deflect TTers. We can get unstuck and ask more because of our wave connections with others that keep pushing against us to change and try NEXT.

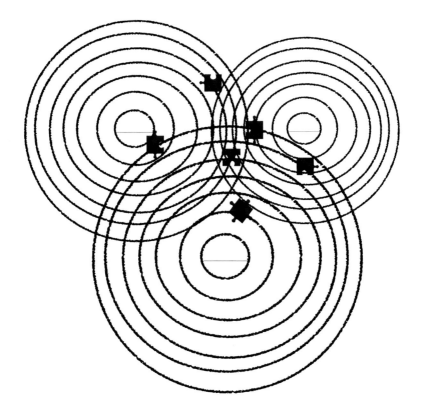

Our connections are showing us more choices and more experidigms with each wave. We get unstuck and expand our boundaries with our connections.

Our wave connections should be expanding upward and outward like these spirals as shown a few pages earlier. The connections expand to infinity as well. We can view these connecting ripples and spirals as a modern day halo around each of us, allowing connections. The original religious halos shown in renaissance religious art were intended to show the connection with the Infinite, and each of us still has them, but we need to put them into use with the Joy equation. Halos connect our "I am…ness".

The TTer and Taker deflection shields help us keep out those who will close our hearts to our "I am…" and our experidigms. We live our life for viewing our "I am…" and in no way live in a voyeuristic "you are…."

Choice Theory

Just as any change has the S-curve shape over time, choices follow a special optimal flow that relates them together in speed and quality to the experidigm. This basic choice diagram relates each component along a vertical access runway. The speed to go up and down is approximately the same speed to go from left to right. This allows each horizontal component of the experidigm to be selected with the same rapid speed while allowing the horizontal components to be compared in key parameters, like quality, price, color, texture, and any design feature.

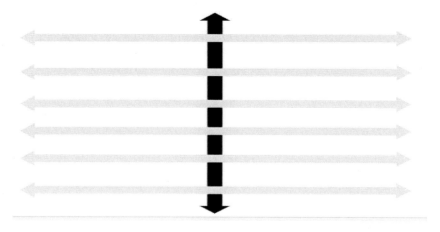

Make selections for each component on a quality scale from high (left) to low (right) and then move on to the NEXT component up or down the vertical experidigm. By making all component selections this way, we arrive at a new experidigm. As we get used to making selections, it takes less and less time for us to make them and we rapidly move to another experidigm. We pick from many different components (on long vertical axis) and in each horizontal component we pick among the many products in each component (from low quality to high quality and related pricing). This selection flow efficiency follows the Constructal Law[9] of nature. The Constructal law basically says that far a system to exist, it must evolve in such a way as to allow easier flow. The selection choice flow for an experidigm will get easier and more efficient over time as practice and sharing experidigms give necessary examples. When each "rib" area is finished take a look how it fits with all ribs along the whole experidigm.

Below are sample selections for a home remodeling experidigm and the types of experts helpful to make selections on each horizontal. For example, on the wall horizontal one must select the color, any picture that goes on the wall, and if any lights will be put on it and for each of these selections we could use a catalog horizontal or an expert. Each horizontal has multiple selections like this wall example. For each component coordinating certain key features like color is very important.

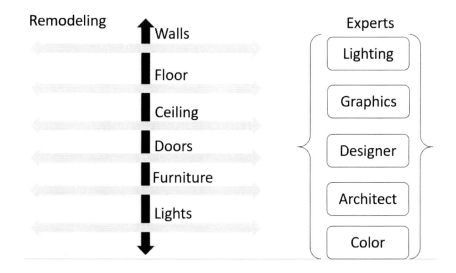

Here below are shown health components for a health experidigm and what selections are required for various times of day. Each component is a part of a health definition.

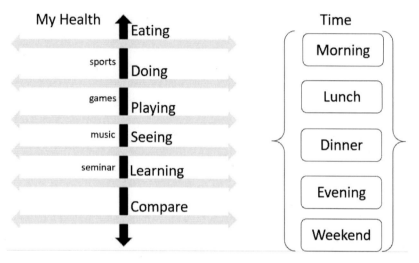

And here below are shown dressing components and the selections required for different events.

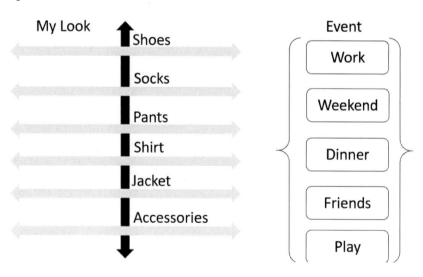

Urgency and Freshness

The choice approach shown above assists with the speed of selection and keeps the decision and selection process moving through all the components: forward, backward, and sideways at maximum speed with easy access to any decision, old or new. This urgency is important to link visualization with the possibilities and options right now. We do not need to procrastinate and say to ourselves, "I need to wait on my whole visualization until this one thing is available (or comes true)." No, use what you have now and build the entire experidigm and experience it. With this experience, you are in a better position to decide what you really need NEXT to perfect the experidigm. We need to live in the act of doing, not just the act of thinking and visualizing, Action creates the necessary joy and connections to which we can respond and build upon.

Urgency creates a freshness in life that is palpable, that adds vivacity to joy. Freshness makes joy feel new. A simple addition or choice to an existing experidigm creates freshness. A new choice everyday creates freshness every day.

Urgency and freshness create openness to the infinite of life coming to you, you actually feeling it and taking what you like. Life is like floating down a river and seeing all the choices on the bank and you float by, selecting the things you like. The NEXT is just waiting up on the river bank for us to try. Floating down many rivers of life gives more choice. Each "I am…" person has a unique river and you can flow with it and see more choices.

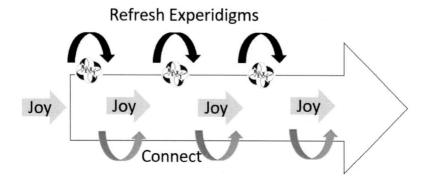

Layers

History builds on itself. Underneath a modern European city is an ancient city, on top of an even more ancient city, on top of farmers' huts, on top of prehistoric campfires. Layer upon layer is added and each layer adds some feature or functionality the previous layer does not have. Humans are the sum of their past plus the experidigm future. Humans stand on the shoulders of the past. Joy is also layered. Each experidigm builds another layer from which to reach higher and explore more joy. Each current layer has the possibility of using all past layers and all future layers. For example, on any given day I walk, I ride a bike, I take my car, I fly in an airplane, and I take a space shuttle. I can do this today, but two hundred years ago I would not have had a car or anything that flies. Joy uses these layers. Each new joy flows from a created experidigm. We share knowledge and build on that. I use the symbolism of connecting waves to show how knowledge is shared with each puzzle piece given.

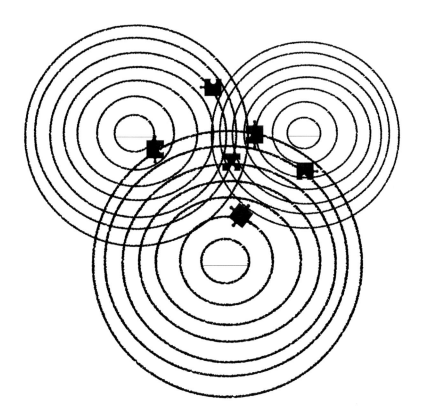

Waves Propagating Choices and Experidigms

In past books, I talked about how spirals and waves connect us with others and allow us to share choices, like puzzle pieces that fit into your Experidigm (see picture above).

In the modern world, if one does not see or touch an "object", one might question whether the object is real or even exists. If the object produces some clear result, we might believe it exists. For instance, since sounds from a radio are heard, listeners believe that radio waves exist. Similarly, seeing images appear on a television screen convinces the watcher that TV waves exist. Participants believe that antennae capture the waves of sight and sound. If we did not have radios and televisions, we might find it hard to believe in radio waves and TV waves. The same is true for mobile phone waves. Conceptually, understanding that waves go from some producing TV or radio station antennae to the local receiving antennae is easy to understand in the big picture because we see it work by turning the TV or radio on. Few people are in the business of creating and managing this wave process, but we believe that it works even though we know almost nothing about it, except to turn the devices on and receive. There are an infinite number of waves and their frequencies.

Would it be so hard to believe that our "I am...ness" creates waves and sends them out to other "I am...s'" antennae to share and connect? You say that is crazy and I am getting a little spooky and spiritual. That is what verbal communication is, sending sound waves to another. Our hearing antennae (i.e. ear) receives the voice wave sound of another and translates the wave sound. Then, one hears and then responds back with a sound wave. The same is true about talking into a phone where a voice sound wave is converted to a digital wave, and then reconverted back to a sound wave for the receiver to hear. Similarly, if we look at someone laughing, we receive sight light waves onto our antennae receptors in the eyes and change them and send them to our brains. One sees them there and understand them there. Obviously, our bodies have many types of antenna that convert the waves the body receives from an external environment to the internal environment in our brain. The brain processes these waves and sends back the responses as waves. Sometimes we send sound waves: sometimes we send "I am..." intention waves. Clearly, one receives sunlight waves all the way from the sun, and our bodies use these waves in many biological processes. Waves can travel long distances and go through physical objects, and combine with other waves to make new waves. Science has shown the attributes of many types of waves we sense and use, although we might take them for granted because we receive waves and translate them effortlessly, without thinking. Some types of waves, like gravity, the effects are felt every second of life, but as of yet, what exactly gravity is, is not known.

Can we send "thought waves" of intentions and aspirations into the external world as waves that can be received by others, understood by the others, and impact others? Of course we can. When we talk, we are sending pressure waves. Many religions and native people practices have believed that our intentions can connect with the Infinite and with other humans and potentially animals – picture American Indians in a circle sharing a pipe to smoke and chanting. Modern spirituality summarizes this belief through what is called the Law of Attraction[10], by becoming "what one believes" because so "as you think, you are". Modern science over the last 50 years have run thousands of experiments and found statistically significant that intentions can be shared over both short distances and long distances[11]. Intentions can be shared, but, of course, you already know this and have experienced sharing intentions. Just like one does not always fully understand what someone else says, we do not always understand the intention of the received message.

One can turn off the "I am..." intention antennae if one wants, just like turning off the TV, or placing blinders on the eyes, or plugs in the ears. One can turn off all of one's antennae and disconnect and insulate himself or herself, like a monk. A "you are..." can say "you are insane listening to ghosts", trying to block another's' "I am..." connections. One can search for the instruction manual to turn on the intention antennae and begin to receive the "I am..." experidigm's intentions of other "I am...s" and the Infinite "I am...." Experidigms can be the intentions being shared.

What would sharing experidigm intentions look like? Just like a TV or radio, the experidigm would look and feel like what was sent, but the receiver gets to determine if reception happens. Did the receiver keep the antennae turned on and was it on the mode or channel to receive the intention? Not every receiver is turned on at every moment. Some are, and can sense and receive and share back. Given an infinite amount of intention experidigms, they need to be understood in the specific context to make sense to the receiver. The Joy equation is one way to make sense of the intentions since the Joy equation is focused on creating joy in the context of a shared experidigm.

The Joy equation is the encoding at the beginning and the end of the experidigm intention message to alert when the specific experidigm intention starts and ends and when another different experidigm or message starts. The context of the experidigm aligns the antennae and the mind to focus the understanding. The more detail of the visual whole experidigm, the better, just like the receiver emits on a TV screen. The mind's-eye as a TV screen is much more enhanced than a two dimensional TV screen. (also, this is why words are too limiting to be shared in these connections.) Not everyone resends and responds to messages -- only those "I am…" who are connected to the specific experidigm wavelength the intention sender is on.

Analytic minds wonder, "How can I understand what the experidigm intentions are saying?" The quick answer is by joining the conversation and connection of the experidigm. It is no different than a normal conversation, saying something to another person, and then misunderstanding. The only way to really get past the misunderstanding is to get more in the context of the experience and keep sharing. Misunderstanding happens all the time in normal communication because words are dependent on context. Saying "I love you" in the bedroom or saying "I love you" at a birthday party mean different things and are related to the context. In the same way, sharing an experidigm intention is only truly understood in the context of the experience. Like most messages, if the message is not understood, and no attempt is made to understand, the message is dropped and ignored like it never happened. The entire purpose of the book *Choosing Up* is to show how to communicate and evolve an experidigm with others. Many approaches and methods are described and illustrated.

The Joy equation sets a clear context for the intention. The beginning of the message says "I am…" and the end says "that is the joy", just like any modern electronic message that has codes at the beginning and end of the message to declare the start and stop of the message. The difference is that an experidigm intention can be a fully 3D dimensional message outside the bonds of time and space in the mind's eye.

Since the message is received in our mind's eye visualization, there is no time or space to contain it. When we try to express it through our space suit, we convert the message to our senses, and use our senses to create waves to share, and then the messages are bounded by time and space as our space suit releases the message.

Our experidigm intention can be sent as far as the experidigm intention wave can flow. If an antenna can receive the intention, then the message made it. If the intention message keeps being sent, then the probability of the intention being received goes up, and so does the probability that the message is understood goes up. Just like TV messages are being sent continuously, but only received and displayed when turned on, an experidigm intention can be sent out and be received, but the understanding is turned off. So keep sending out experidigms intentions – they can be received, understood, and responded to effectively.

Receiving a response from an experidigm can be so joyful. Other "I am…s" will share and connect. The first time connection can be awkward, like talking for the first time with someone new and in the new language of the experidigm. Similar to learning a new foreign language, the mind's eye learns to talk and connect with an experidigm. When we learn a foreign language we talk and listen in the context of actions, and put the meaning in the context of that action and learn in the terms of the experience. We learn the experidigm in the context of the action. Here are a few ways to share intentions:

1) Realize that what the sender sees in their mind's eye is converted to word language and then spoken to the receiver and then converted to the mind's eye, with a lot lost in translation.

2) The sender uses imagery to show the experidigm and more is understood.

3) The sender uses wave intentions to the mind's eye of the receiver similar to the Law of Attraction.

Just as we bring judgments, biases, and culture to our word language, we bring those similar judgments to receiving experidigm intentions. Judgments will translate the intention differently than originally sent. This is good and bad. Good in that this may bring more creativity and more joy to the intention experidigm and grow the experidigm in a new and better way. Bad in the sense that it may cause confusion and disconnection. Any connection has this good and bad. The only way to convert the good and the bad into more good or all good is to keep sharing and trying to understand the context of the experidigm, and when that context is shared more good flows and more joy is created. Clearly TTers and Takers can easily break the connections and insert their "problem" distortions into the connections and try to make their "you are…" delusion the context of reality.

How easy is it to create a distortion? Look at the world and count how many "you are…" comments are received via radio and TV waves. Yes, waves can be sent as "I am…" or "You are…." Know that many lists or definitions are delusions of the "you are…" world to define people. The "I am…" is based on sharing the context of the "I am…:" experidigm, and not to define another and then control them. Our "I am…" does not receive lists; it receives experidigms and creates experidigms in a much deeper and more personal way. All has been created, so one gets what he or she can accept. Open up your antennae and receive joy via evolving experidigms. Be aligned to all "I am…s". The infinite flow offers to everyone; you choose to use choice or not.

The best judgment is for the "I am…" to receive additions to the experidigm and decide whether to accept them or not. Select what you wish. Like any conversation, one chooses what he or she wants to do and how to react. It is best to keep pointing to what joy you want to receive. Keep selecting in the direction of "I am…" expanding. Selection keeps the conversation and connection going. As long as the conversation and connection flows, the joy flows. If the conversation is lost, one can start the conversation anew. In between conversation, imagine working on your experidigms.

Joy is Not

Joy is not an emotion with duality like love-hate, happy-sad, or smile-frown. One has joy or not. Joy is a flow toward an experidigm while being connected. Joy exists within an individual or as part of connected group. The joy is related to how connected one is and what the flow of the exper-idigm is. The creativity, joy and love of the "I am…" is always shared. "I am…" is and are connected. One's joy wave hits another person and adds to them.

Joy is not experienced in a "you are…" moment. One might feel power, control, dominance, winning competitive advantage in your taking "you are…," but that is not joy. That is the unconnected taking and thinking that taking has some value. The only delusional value "you are…" persons have is in their own false" survivor delusion they must take from and hurt their victims to survive. They have chosen this "you are…" connectedness, and forfeited their 'I am…" creativity.

Joy looks like a school of fish turning together, a flock of birds coordinated in a "V", a hive of bees working together, a line of ants bringing food to the nest, birds nesting on the cliff, trees bending in the sunny wind, or seals on a rocky beach. Joy is a connected experience. Joy comes when connections flow to the experidigm. Instead of standing on the river bank and watching the flow go by, get into the flow (with you, a boat, your connections, and all things) NOW-ASAP. No reason to postpone flow. Get out of the recurring cycle, the Taker cycle and get into the flow.

PART 3:

Connected Life

Perspectives in Life

"I am..." because I free will "I am…," and I connect to the Infinite and all infinite "I am....s" We are made by our thoughts and our will, and we are the sum of our experiences as we change experidigms as time passes. Our thoughts have a habit of wandering through the infinite, connecting with the Infinite, sharing the love and respect built into the fabric of the infinite. Left alone, our thoughts and words can bind us and construct a prison around us, thinking others are different and negative and hurtful. Alone and unconnected, we drift away from the "I am..." creative connection.

What does connection mean in relation to the Joy equation? The word connection does not contain all the meaning and action of connecting "I am…s." Connecting includes a jumble of words all at once: loving, caring, sharing, cooperating, helping, teamwork, and any positive way to say "we are together heling each other." In this simple picture below the "I am…" positive connection is on the right and negative "you are…" hurt is on the left. When one hears the left side, deflect and think on the right side.

The simple word "connection" is trying to convey a sense of active participation and sharing knowledge in a positive, up-lifting, and encouraging way to contribute to the NEXT experidigm transition of people. Love is the respect to connect with another "I am…." The opposite of love, anger and argumentation, means internalizing the bad thoughts of another, so deflect bad thoughts and get back to your "I am…" and sharing love.

The purpose of connecting is to get new perspectives or knowledge from different kinds of people who do not all think alike. Divergent thinking is received by the experidigm in the spirit of openness, choice, and discussion, and for decision of the "I am…ness" for appropriateness. Connecting is not necessarily building a relationship that is focused on emotional or support needs (like a mother with a baby or the government giving to the poor), but for knowledge, choice, and growth needs. Connection is not about empathy, but is a sharing of expertise and experience. Connection is somewhat impersonal focused on meaningful progress to the pointing after experidigm, using care and love for the process, and shared belief of getting to the experidigm and overcoming any and all delusional fear. Joy comes from the flow. These connections are constantly being changed and updated depending on the flow and what is needed (skills, material, money, people, etc.) for the specific experidigm being sought. Just like sports teams are constantly changing with tactics, strategy, and associated personnel, an experidigmer adds new connections for tactics and strategy.

If one does not have connections, the experidigms are limited to only an individual's perceptions, accumulated learning (if any), and experiences (if any). The diversity of a large group is eye opening, shedding a light in the darkness. Fear can be a solitary friend. As we look into the darkness of future change alone, we do not know how far the imagined fall and hurt will be, but connections know and can lead one through the imagined fall.

Interestingly, I rarely use the word "relationship" to describe these type of experidigm connections because relationships come with extra status quo baggage and stagnation and addiction to keep the relationship the way it is—and trying to keep it that way forever. Relationships are similar to living organisms' symbiotic with another living organism — good, but not necessarily helpful (but potential to be) in reaching up to a new experidigm. Experidigms flow from a creative "I am...," not a stagnation or addictive relationship that is like glue that keeps one in the here and now. Relationships should not be confused with an experidigm, and building relationships should never be an experidigm in and of itself.

The intent of the connection is mainly focused on how and what one can contribute to one's own "I am..." experidigm or to another's "I am..." experidigm. Connection is active listening and providing knowledge and experience. Reciprocity and synergy flow from connections as one day the recipient is the receiver and vice versa. The roles depend on the need of the experidigm being explored and shared and the amount of creativity in the flow

Obviously, the intentional negativity of a "you are…" Taker will hurt and eventually destroy creative "I am…" connections. Less obvious is when "criticism" and "why" questions flip from being helpful fact learning questions to negative judgments intended to harm connections and "I am… ness." 'Why" questions to another can start down a very slippery slope of negative judgment. Negative judgment more than challenges "I am…" creativity and wants to stifle that creativity with stagnation. Implied in some methods of "why" criticism is that since the answer is not accepted by the critic, the associated thought/action/person is not accepted, and the defining "you are…" then comes from the critic to entrap, and imprison the "I am…' in the "you are..." of the critic's making. The critic then replies "who me, I was only asking a question." In reality, the defining as "you are..." was intended and will be reinforced with more why questions.

When one hurts another, since we are all connected, that one also hurts himself or herself, and limits both capabilities and ability to reach higher experidigms. "You are…:" and negative criticism hurt our connections. Competition can also hurt connections. Competition in the quest for playing and/or associated with games normally is not hurtful to connections and can enhance connections with learning. Playful and game competition can put one in the flow of joy to a paradigm and not hurt another. However, competition for **limited** resources (i.e. materials, geography/land, thoughts, inventions, concepts like love and money and God), can lead to hoarding and dominance intentionally hurtful to sharing connections. Cooperation is more common than competition in nature – flocks of birds, schools of fish, clusters of trees, hives of bees, etc. Of course, nature has predators that eat other beings, but even these predators do not hoard and store their "wealth" and use the stored "wealth" power to totally eliminate their predator victims. Nature does not seem to hoard or be wasteful. In nature, life thrives through cooperation and support to overcome life's challenges (i.e. bad weather, famine, etc.) as opposed to a predator "survival of the fittest' as the main evolving route. Sure, evolution favors life forms that can adapt to and overcome life's challenges, not because they employ "you are..." taking, but because they use cooperative "I am...ness.

Realize that a person's attitudes have an impact on all connected people, so embrace all people and respect them for their cooperative and connected "I am...ness." You say, "I have an impact on others?" Yes, the individual "I am...ness" adds to the collective joy of "I am...ness," or the individual "you are..." hurts the group "I am...." Even ones status quo stagnation hurts the group "I am...."

Sharing Spirit

Having a good attitude when connecting allows the "I am..." connection and two-way sharing. The sharing has many aspects:

+ as a teacher

+ as one who is learning

+ as one who is trading value

+ as a helper and giver or receiver

+ as an expert offering insight

+ assisting in supporting experidigm creation

+ in fun and play

+ in general, to contribute to growth

Sharing allows another to witness another perspective in love, non-judgment, and respect. Only share to the amount needed, no reason to horde and stockpile excess "profit" because always evolve to the NEXT better state where the excess is not needed. While sharing, one is independent in one's "I am…", but understands the common moral good, and supports and witnesses to the NEXT level to which one is aspiring.

Danger Being Defined

Words describing us tend to define us in terms of how others perceive us, more on a doing or action basis, than who we really are, what our experiences are, and what we want. When people describe us, they summarize us in to a limited elevator pitch that contains only a fraction of whom we are and what we will be. Anything more they say would "be too confusing". "So, keep it simple." For example, here are some words to describe us:

+ for business: customer, client, supplier, consumer, buyer, accountant, sales representative.

+ for doing: carpenter, lawyer, doctor, driver, etc.

+ for societal role: politician, religious leader, police, etc.

+ for relationships: father, son, boss, worker, etc.

+ for type: leader, servant, jerk, liar, etc.

Although there are thousands of words to describe us and an infinite number of combinations, we use very few. And we mainly use those words that just convey what we do for work, like, "I am an accountant". We respond the same like "I am an artist." We let others use that summary to say they know us. They use words to describe us, but they really do not know us, and we may feel it is not polite to correct them. This process of describing who we are is not very good, and we are not very patient with it. How can we connect with others if we do not say who we are very well? It is harder to share if we do not have an understanding of who the other person is and what he or she wants? Perhaps we should spend more time saying who we are and what we want.

As if you did not know, I am an Experidigmer – one who connects with those different from me and builds my experiences of my NEXT, best future. I share my NEXT picture of the future with as much detail as possible so others can participate and improve the NEXT. I am not described by what I do now, but by what I point to, the entire picture of what I point to, and it is not stagnant. My future picture is always changing, so I must share the changes with my connections. I am not defined by what I share or do. In fact, I am not defined in a little box because I have so many experiences that I am growing and integrating. I am spiritual; I am a learner; I am a traveler; I am a business builder; I am a sharer; though I have many dimensions, I am adding more.

Defining you has a danger associated with it. You may find yourself trapped in that definition and unable to get out. You can become unconnected once you get defined.

The danger of being defined by yourself or a "you are..." is that you accept it. Accepting the definition will limit how you see the world, and you will fit yourself into that limited view. More and more you become more comfortable with that view and block out most other views. You decide to not change. You view the world in a duality of what you are, and how others are different – black and white, republican and democrat, rich or poor. Once you accept a definition, you attract people just like you. All they see, feel, or do are very similar to what you see, feel, or do. This acceptance of being defined will be hard to change. As they say, "Once a ???, always a ???." Put any action definition in the blank to describe the situation.

You say hogwash! I have my work life, my family life, and my social life. It is good that you have all these lives, but in each role there is a very high probability that you live each as defined and rarely evolve in any of them, except to have time pass. For example, at work I am a sales rep; to my family, I am dad, and to my friends I am a state football fan and watch them all the time. That is what you do, to where are you evolving? What is your Joy experidigm in each area and how do you combine them into your whole person and share that with others? Without an experidigm to share with your connections, you will be the SAME TOMORROW AS YOU ARE TODAY UNTIL YOU DIE. Of course you will experience random events, but your "I am..." has not been explored, nor have you experienced the creative Infinite. If that is what you are defined as, that is dangerous to your space suit.

Many people set goals, and do move forward and change and improve. This is OK, but this change is normally defined in terms of a doer "goal" definition – "I want to go from an accountant degree to a CPA then to a firm partner". This is a very well-defined goal path. Once again, these goals are OK, but they do not show a visual experidigm of your future that others can connect with, share with you, add to, and achieve with you. All doer goal definitions are limiting, no matter how much you get paid and how many people work for you. You might feel better getting paid more money, but that does not really increase your Joy equation – it is difficult to buy meaningful connections and experiences. Buying a prostitute is doing sex, not love.

People identify so much with their goals and descriptions, they begin to keep score and compare themselves with others to see it they score better by attaining more status, more power and more money. Are you the best in your doer description? Sorry, that was a trick question. Does it really matter that you are the best in your limited description that others pin on you and you accept? It does not matter. You were born with the best and Infinite "I am..." the Infinite could give you. Use it to make the most joyful experiences and connections, not to collect money or pin medals on your chest.

Pride and confidence may give you temporary rewards, but these are the limitations of the trapped life, living in the jail cell of need for "you are..." acceptance of your defined role. This is worse than slavery because you falsely believe you are your description and that is it; that is all you have. At least slaves know they are not physically free, and they picture their future when they are in their perfect joy world. They fight and long for freedom. In our modern world, unfortunately, some accept our modern slavery to the "you are..." definition given and marketed to us. People accept their "you are..." slavery because they have imprisoned their 'I am..." experidigms and "I am..." connections. Later, we will talk about accepting modern day compliancy addiction.

Lucky for us all, the defined slavery is easy to mentally overcome, just by remaining connected to your "I am..." and reaching for your NEXT experidigm. To combat being defined, you must make your own visual experidigm of the future, and free yourself by connecting with other "I am... ers" to reach and leap up growing to your whole experidigm.

I am not suggesting to fight, challenge, or argue with anyone who gives you a defined tag as to whom you are. No arguing because that means your "I am..." loses. Instead, when someone says, "you are a _____," this is your opportunity to say, "Let me share my whole experidigm." You always have the ability to say "I am..." and here is my current experidigm, and would you like to add to my experidigm? You can break free from other people's definitions and promote your experidigm.

Many times people will ask one to give them the summary of their life because the asker does not have time to listen, to learn, to care, to understand whom one really is and whom they are becoming. Frankly, the askers are just lazy and really interested mainly in their own life. They ask for the part of a life as if the parts tell the whole story. Being asked to simplify and define your life so another "you are..." can define you and put you in a box is not in your best interest. When asked to summarize and define and simplify, always give a picture of your experidigm because if they really hear that and care, they can participate. Give them a chance to participate in your experidigm.

"I am... actioning"

An experidigm is the action picture of the "I am…" will. Examples are "I am doing…," "I am building…," "I am creating…," and "I am actioning… of any kind." The experidigm is an invitation to other creative "I am…s" to join in with your experidigm and participate now, because the "I am doing…." is happening now and being manifest now. Saying "I am actioning…" makes the future happen now. The "I will…" becomes the "I am…" as one proclaims the "I am…." The "I will…" is a dream; the "I am…" is happening now and has been willed into existence from all "I am…ness".

The experidigm is the wholeness of the action, not just a part. If one cannot visualize the whole right now, then what we have now is good enough to experidigm, and we will add to it. Just picture your experidigm and get started doing and acting for your joy. This is very important. Others suggest saying what "I am…' is (usually in positive way), and that it will come true. This is ok, but has the defining oneself problem (and getting stagnant or addicted to the definition). The lack of clarity of what the word really means (versus the holistic visual experidigm) is limiting. Here is an example of breaking the "I am…" into parts -- "I am – insert word: prosperous, successful, victorious, talented, creative, wise, healthy, happy, in shape, passionate, strong, confident, attractive, secure, kind, or any other positive word. The truth is each "I am…" is already ALL of these positive words and much more when flowing toward and doing one's "I am…" experidigm in a connected way. The experidigm contains all of these positive words and the whole joy of the experience with all "I am…s." Listing all the words you want to be is only a start, but be careful. The words may become stagnant or addictive "you are…ness."

The experidigm is "not of the world, but in and beyond the world." The purpose of life is to have joy in this world as "I am…s" connect with experidigms. "I am…" is always doing and evolving, whether physical, mental or spiritual or all three simultaneously.

Adjusting Your Joy

Life is not perfect. I bet you noticed this. Just because you have an experidigm does not mean it will happen immediately or at all. Nor should it happen because you may have already evolved to a different place. An experidigm is not a goal to achieve by a certain time nor is any stress attached to it. By having an experidigm, you have engaged the "I am..." connections and the Infinite and the law of attraction starts to work and bring things for you to receive. You begin evolving but see more and learn more. You make shifts in your direction and see better experidigms. The more you experience, the more you know you need to experience. Never get frustrated. Your perfect experidigm does not happen exactly the way you visualize it because you are on the path to an even better one.

This is not goal setting, so there is no such thing as failure to achieve your experidigm. You may fail a goal, but you never fail an experidigm – the Infinite 'I am...' just offers the NEXT experidigm. Only you judge your choices on the way to your experidigm. No reason to throw stones at yourself. The world wants you to define yourself and set goals. Ok, but you have more than definitions and goals – you have experidigms and connections. Let your "I am..." learn and create the best for you. Do not rely on shallow goal setting.

A Story – Always More

It was parent career day at school and the kids were excited to hear what other parents did. Maybe one day the kids could grow up and be just like one of the parents: do what they do and be defined like them. All they really need to do is to pick one and learn, work hard at it, live it and the students will be defined and accepted by people around them. When the day was done, everyone had to tell the teacher which job they wanted. The teacher was happy until she came to little Johnny. Little Johnny was confused. He wanted all he saw and more. He was thinking big. He did not want to be one of these forever, so he told the teacher he wanted them all and more. Johnny was scolded and was put in the corner to think and told to select just one. Johnny sat in the corner visualizing how he could be all of them. He knew he could be all of them. He smiled. He told the teacher he would be President. She said "you are too stupid, so pick something else." Johnny smiled. He spent the day in the corner. Johnny grew into his experidigms. Johnny did not accept his definition cage.

What would you do?

A Story – Another Road

A person comes to an intersection and there are five ways to go. Fearing going the wrong way and getting lost, the person goes back and never returns. Another person comes and immediately takes a road. Eventually, he or she comes back and takes another road. Again he or she returns and takes yet another road. Though never returning to the original starting point, the traveler takes another road, then another road after another after another road. The traveler is still taking another road today.

Will you take another road?

Space Suit Connecting

We all have the same standard-issue space suit with skin, basic human body operation and shape, and the limiting five senses. This space suit is a machine that has a limited operating life like any machine that has ever been created. It has a limited physical operating range. In addition, like all machines, our machine has a purpose. The purpose is to house and contain our "I am..." which is connected to the Infinite and all other "I am...s" who are connected to the Infinite.

Our senses are only related to working with and operating our temporary space suit, in much the same way car engine sensors suggest what might be happening in the car engine. Human senses do not really "know" what is happening, they are just reporting ranges to the 'I am...' for the "I am..." to interpret and use, if it so chooses. Our 'I am...' can use or misuse the senses in any way our "I am..." wants. We have free will to choose to believe the external world is what it appears to be. We also have the free will to choose if the internal "I am..." imagination is real in the external world or if we choose to make our internal world real in the external world. Yes, our 'I am...' will can impact the external world, and make experidigms happen. The "you are..." will comes to me only through my senses—I can choose to ignore it and only use my "I am..." will.

Does anything come into my "I am..." beyond the use of my senses? My imagination does. My visualizations do. Miracles do. By definition, miracles are beyond the senses and my body machine. Miracles are my "I am..." connection to the infinite creative forces of the Infinite. With the Infinite, I can imagine and visualize and bring into my external world what my "I am..." expects to be joyful. I can sense the joyful experidigm I bring into the world. The Infinite can sense the experidigm I bring into the world. Others connected with the Infinite can sense my experidigm and make their "I am..." joy discernment. The connected world can share my joy of the experidigm, or not -- their will dictates what their "I am..." accepts.

I can make as many experidigms as I want, and I can share them with the external world as long as my space suit is connected to the external world. The Infinite can experience my experidigms though my senses. Just like we watch a TV, the Infinite can experience all connected individuals experidigms.

Addiction is Becoming Unconnected

For so many reasons, we can choose to think it is our individual passion to do by ourselves because others are so hard to work with (i.e. different opinions and points of view) or they are just hurtful (i.e. TTers, and Takers). And, as we know, if we let their hurtful ways into our "I am...," we can really become an unconnected "you are...." We know we can get rid of a "you are..." by getting connected with one "I am..." and other "I am...s." It is hard to snap out of being a "you are…" by just relying on oneself.

We can build a wall around ourselves and focus internally and appear to be living. Any chart or program that suggests a person evolves through a series of levels from basic survival to spiritual connection is just an artificial creation. Striving to live for varying times in each level as we seemingly "progress" through life is also artificial. Putting oneself in one of these levels is artificial. These levels are "you are..." creations and only exist if you allow them to exist and let them in your "I am...." These levels are a fabrication and delusional observation of a "You are…" classification. Any system that attempts to classify you is a delusional "you are..." system meant to manipulate your thinking (and in the case of 3rd party rules, to control you). Your journey in life is not through these levels or any other levels. Levels do not exist within your "I am...." The Infinite exists within your 'I am..." and you can learn to experience it and connect with it. You can choose what you want from the Infinite to create your experiences. The real issue is not an artificial hierarchy classification, but that you are trying to be unconnected and attempting to justify where you are in life because of these "safe" classifications. You say to yourself, "so it is." Addiction occurs when we get unconnected and stuck in repeating internally an "ok" habit. Addiction is not joy.

We have discussed the value of being connected as to enable and enlarge each visualization and searching for each of your experidigms. You will always be evolving to your NEXT experidigm when you are connected. You know you are connected when you keep getting signals, information, and friction from all of your connections. They are participating in your growth evolution. When connections stop, you do not have this productive friction and your choices are made in isolation from your "I Am..." – you are stuck in "you are..." domination which does not allow anyone in to help change you. Your "you are..." demands to be fed the same something, over and over again. Being unconnected, you cannot create and just take what you know, over and over again. This is addiction. Normally we think addition is about drugs or some other stimulate (i.e. sex, money, etc.), and it can be. It can also be getting stuck in a routine of life and just repeating it -- we are addicted to the safe routine. Routine is being addicted to the unconnected life. The good thing is that connecting to the Infinite snaps you out of stagnation and routine, leaving addiction behind you as other "I am...s" participate in your active experidigm life.

Being stuck, not flowing to the NEXT experience, is addictively dangerous. We become so comfortable and content with the definitions around us, the labels we can give ourselves (or those "you are..." labels), that we become them and only them. We stop growing; we stop "I am...ing." We become the definitions our mind accepts, and we keep repeating them over and over, until they become our wall to keep "I am..." growth in a prison cell, allowing no connections. People say, "I select this level in the Maslow hierarchy and others have done that, and so that is OK with me." "My job is perfect for me. I go to work every day, I am called a "whatever," and I can be a "whatever" for the rest of my life." "I do not need more education (i.e. learning). I know enough, and besides, I am tired. Most days, I get home, eat, watch some TV, and go to bed." "I get unstuck and unwind on my vacation once or twice a year."

The physical "You are…" world reality is that society accepts when you are addicted to that which society wants. The constant drone hidden behind the surface is, "please, just fit in and do your part to maintain the status quo." If you do not fit in, society may classify you and attack and may even drug you to fit in, like excited school kids who are labeled as disturbers and need to take drugs to behave as expected. Some school children are prescribed drugs to control their attention deficit disorders. I remember when my child was in an early grade at school. The teacher asked questions in class, and my child was so excited to answer he proudly blurted the answers out loud. He loved learning and participating. Eventually the teacher did not like this way of answering. This answering out load needed to be eliminated. Something needed to be done so the teacher could retain control and my son could keep a positive spirit of learning.

The issue here was not my son. The issue was that the local school had not created strategies to assist enthusiastic students to connect in the classroom. The answer should not be to single out one student, but to find a better way of connecting the students in the class to the discussion and ensuring the connective discussion happens in an open and experidigm way. In this case, I suggested to the teacher that my son will raise his hand and wait to be called on before he answered out loud. I spoke with my son, and he agreed. All the future connections were ok. He learned an incredible amount and had a great education and the teacher was able to focus on the lesson. This simple story demonstrates what can happen if we are led down a right path that allows connection; always work to get connected again to "I am...." Choose methods to connect and avoid methods that cause stagnation or addiction, like drugs.

Our "I am..." is designed to connect. The connection carries love and trust, and because of this, we trust. When we sense a "you are..." or hear a "you are..." realize you are about to be disconnected, so never trust a "you are..." type statement.

The issue is that by not figuring out how to connect in a positive way, and by creating an addiction to prevent connection, society encourages the addiction. Society more than tolerates addiction; it can enforce rules and laws and drug people to ensure the addiction. The status quo wants to stay in comfort and is content to stay in addictive passive comfort, fighting change.

Addiction occurs when you get stuck and cannot connect to get out and back to your "I am...." If we accept this addiction, we accept a "you are..." that society has thrust upon us. Society creates these addictions to keep one compliant with the status quo. The good news is that you can snap your fingers and break free and use your "I am..." to connect and explore your NEXT paradigm.

Stuck with Complacency

As I have alluded to, sometimes we are not stuck because we are artificially and delusionally addicted, but because we are just outright complacent. We just do not really care- to move, to learn, to do, or to connect. We just take life for granted and surround ourselves with people who just take the same way of life for granted. We miss the infinite connection and we miss experidigms. We miss the flow of life. We just keep doing the same things over and over again: watching TV, going to the same restaurants, doing the same things.

A bold step is needed to break out of complacency. You need to develop connections. The act of thanking people, doing actions, and creating with those around you catapults you into appreciation and understanding and back to the journey and exploration of "I am...." Just saying thank you opens you up to explore and receive and involve those around you, reconnecting. Saying "thank you" engages the Infinite and reignites involvement.

"Thank you" enables moving together while appreciating the involvement of others and continuing to encourage involvement. Thank you shows you understand and can build forward.

"Thank you, but..." allows you to direct your conversation in the direction you want to move. You can move the conversation toward your experidigm and what you need to explore. A series of "thank you, but..." can have you arrive at a new place, sharing that place with the person. You leave complacency behind. By saying thank you, movement has already happened and enough movement can move you beyond complacency.

Be thankful for any action or observation that gets you going:

+ showing

+ sharing

+ listening

+ talking

+ caring

+ doing

You are the director of your theatrical play, and thank all your actors. Thanks for the action, the music, the love, and the connection to produce your play. Working all day and sitting in front of a TV all night is not a play.

Interestingly, when humans are confronted with death, and a limited time to live, many have regrets. Here are some of those regrets:

+ Did what was "expected" of me, and did not pursue my dreams

+ Spent too much time doing unimportant things, like over time at work and watching TV.

+ Wished I had stated my opinions more instead of hiding them

+ Wished I had stay connected with friends instead of unimportant things

+ Needed to focus on joy, not ego, privilege, or fitting in

When I hear these statements, I cry. A non-stagnant, joyful life follows the Joy equation and focuses on experidigms and "I am..." connections. No regrets from this focus.

Journey Mapping

Life is not a journey with an end goal with signals along the way to let the traveler know he or she is going in the right direction. That is a project plan for achievement at work, not life. Life is many experiences, each as the core of joy and shared with love to be felt by all who share. One experience might be a project, but that is such a small part of the experiences of life. Joy is found in living experidigms.

Seeing life as a journey with an ultimate destination is an excuse to stay on the same path, like one is addicted to the journey. People can get addicted to the journey. When someone sells a journey, be very careful that the journey does not become habit forming. In a journey the end is supposed to be the joy. With an experidigm the experience, sharing and connecting are part of the joy. (note: see Part 8)

Net Experidigmer Score

The end number for the Joy equation just needs to be positive and rising, an indication that one is finding joy and not stagnating. The total magnitude of the number has NO meaning either as comparative to other people or to some high number as better. People are all different, so any magnitude has no meaning. A joy number of 5 can be equal to a joy number of 1000 for another person. Never get caught up in the number as if keeping score is important. With joy and love we are not competing, we are loving and sharing.

Similarly, how does one know they are progressing well with their experidigms? If progress is made with our experidigms, the joy score will go up. Make progress with evolving experidigms. Instead of getting too mathematical, just ask yourself, on a scale from 1 (bad) to 10 (good), how do I feel about my current experidigm experience progress? If feel like anywhere from 4 to 7, progress is being made, so keep pointing and evolving with that experidigm. Spend more time choosing and connecting. If between 8 and 10, make plans for a major change in the experidigm to reach and point further. This prevents getting too comfortable and addicted. Joy occurs as we flow and evolve, so evolve from a point of strength. On the other hand, the range from 1 to 3 requires a complete overhaul and redo of the experidigm. Get new connections and explore new avenues for your joy.

This net experidigmer score from 1 to 10 is a very broad question to check to see if your joy is evolving. Also, ask your team members this question and see how they rank you. This will protect you from becoming complacent and self-serving with you own answer.

Becoming Experidigmers

All that is needed to become an experidigmer is a picture of your future and taking the first action and choice to get to that picture. NEXT, just announce the experidigm to others so they can assist you and get connected.

A Day Connected

All days connected and sharing the experidigm are joyful.

First, acknowledge in the "I am…:" that you are ready to receive all that comes to enhance the experidigm. Point toward the experidigm and take the first step and make new choices.

Second, try something new and share the results with the team and talk about the NEXT new thing. Ask the "I am…" team to suggest more appropriate choices. Try the new choices that make sense to you. Keep looking for more choices.

Third, thank all "I am…" for their thoughts and wisdom.

Not Religion or Politics

History normally records the actions, not the choices, one makes as one flows with and to one's experidigms. The choices are kept in the mind's eye and are personal. Choices are made as the experience flows, not in isolation, but connected. The choices stand outside of politics and religion and are based on the positive "I am…." Politics is based on "you are…" status quo and should not be used to make choices. Some religions use fear and "you are…" definitions to prevent the "I am…" from making good moral choices.

Base choices on the 'I am…" that fit with your experidigm, and discussions with other "I am…ers."

PART 4:

Healing – No Walls

Beyond the Senses

Our "I am…" is beyond the senses and controls our ability to connect and experience the world, to create our experidigms. Our space suit is worldly bound and uses our "I am…" for direction if we allow our "I am…" to connect. If we get unconnected (by "you are…"), we then only rely on our space suit and senses and these are easily deluded. If everyone is disconnected, everyone is deluded. Being part of the group delusion leaves you in the same place – living in your delusion. Being part of the group delusion has no benefits.

But you say, "I am just following" the wisdom of the day…." Yes, it appears the "you are…" has helped you make this excuse so that you can fit in to the stagnant status quo. Being part of mass hypnosis and delusion does not make it any better because others do it. You have the "I am…" choice that leads to healing and wholeness. I am so that I am.

The space suit is so influential to one's "I am…" that the "I am…" believes what the space suit reports to it as the space suit sees, hears, and feels the external world. However, the space suit is a machine, an awesome machine that only operates in a range, and only interprets the world in that certain range. The word "interpret" is most important here. We interpret the world is flat because as far as we can see, the world is flat. So human space suits thought for thousands of years the world was flat. Now we know the world to be a sphere. What we think is real, may not be real. Our senses just interpret the world near us like any animal. Our senses do not gather all the information around us, and they do not store everything they sense. Our space suit machine interprets and stores only a small portion of the changing external reality.

Instead of having to interpret everything, people begin to share information and must make judgments about the truthfulness of what they are hearing and seeing. Some ideas we believe from others are easily proven true just by looking at the physicality of them – an airplane view of the earth shows the earth as a sphere. Other ideas others tell us may not be as easily proven, like "work hard and get ahead." These ideas that are beyond the senses, the "I am…" can use the mind's eye to create experidigms and a way to live in the changing now. Individuals use their "I am…" to make selections and choices to create the reality of their experidigms.

Unfortunately, when "you are…" statements become the belief of society and the masses, a mass delusion can exist and seem real. Slavery is a clear example. Society created and accepted laws that a person could be owned. Slavery only exists where the mass delusion makes it so and the "you are…" Taker benefits economically. Similarly, modern day advertising can create false delusions like we can "open happiness" by drinking caffeinated sugar water -- this mass delusion can lead to a realty of mass diabetes and severe health issues. The "I am…:" can get trapped by a false delusion intentionally created by TTers or Takers. Many illnesses are delusions created and supported by our minds that we make real, and our space suit just makes them real by continuing to operate with the delusion as though it is real.

Delusions or Experidigms

The delusions of sickness, fear, and lack are a direct result of being disconnected from your "I am..." and all "I am....s." The 'I am...' is always here and now, but that does not mean we accept it and recognize it. That does not mean we "let it be." The power of "I am..." to create and live in joy is absolute and forever. Unfortunately, we can create sickness, fear, and lack on our own and believe these delusions actually exist. It is like sitting in a dark room and saying and believing that light does not exist. We create the darkness in our mind. Light exists no matter what our minds think. The apparent disappearance of light to our senses is a sensual space suit delusion because light does exist, and through our connections and experidigms we recognize it and allow it and give it space and acknowledge it. Light is just awaiting our recognition of it, and we allow it. If we recognize darkness, we have darkness. If we recognize light, we have light. Darkness is a problem created by our minds.

Like darkness, fear is an individual delusion and group delusion. Fear is a problem. Like all Taker problems, the problem draws away the "I am..." and keeps taking and taking and taking and trying to keep both an individual and a society in the Taker cycle. Fear does not exist. Instead, the "I am..." knows love and love is just awaiting it's recognition by our "I am..." and connection with all "I am...." Our "I am..." creates space for our love related experidigm. Our love experidigm is always in us and connected, and we just need to recognize it and bring it creatively out the way we want it to appear in our space suit life.

Lack of prosperity and abundance is another delusion. Like a dark room, we sit in a room with nothing, no prosperity. Yet, this room is of our space suit making. Snap out of it. Acknowledge your "I am..." and take action toward your Experidigm, making positive choices and connecting with those who assist with their "I am...ness." Prosperity happens as joy flows from the experidigm.

Sickness is part of the dark, lacking, fearing space suit room. It is a family member of the all the delusions that an unconnected "I am..." causes. Sickness can result from living in our parts world and believing that parts are what matter. The parts can be disconnected and cause problems. If we eat poorly, we get poor health. If we exercise poorly, we get poor health. If we get stress, we get poor health. Our poor "you are..." delusions weaken us and lead to poor health. A strong and connected "I am..." with a healthy experidigm can prevent and fight disease and win. Pursuing an experidigm is positive therapy. Sickness is a Taker problem, and keeps you in the Taker cycle and keeps telling you what to do in the delusion and keeps taking your value as you do the delusion. Health is the recognition of our wholeness in the "I am..." and our "I am..." can acknowledge and accept this wholeness. We can welcome wholeness and we are wholeness. "I am..." accepts wholeness. A great experidigm is to accept your wholeness.

In a world where "I am..." people connect beyond the space suit, with the Infinite "I am...," healing can happen. History is replete with examples. Every example shows the connection of "I am..." looking into a future wholeness experidigms. The future health wholeness must be in your "I am..." to accept it, so put it there and will it – it is your "I am..." creative connection power to do that. Create and ask. Ask the Infinite "I am..." to create your health experidigm.

If you do not create the health experidigm, you will wander in the dark, fearing, lightless room. Yes, other "I am...s" can grab you and get you out of the dark room, but you still have to create your health will at some point. Healing occurs when you align with your wholeness "I am...." and wholeness "I am...." of others and the Infinite "I am...." "I am...." Yes, it takes your experidigm will and more – the connections of other "I am...s." We have all experienced the miracle of wholeness at least once in our lives, but we should live in the joy of wholeness all the days of our lives.

One day our space suit is just all used up. The space suite stops, and we stay connected to the "I am...." Our "I am...." goes onto another experidigm without the delusional senses and this temporary space suit. Our "I am... ness" is always part of "I am...ness" at any time no matter what space suit we have at the time.

Science and medicine are an experidigm. They are a creation of our 'I am...' will. Like all experidigms, they are part of our evolution and hopefully part of our Joy equation. Not all experidigms lead to joy. Experidigms get old and an old experidigm is not an experidigm any longer and can lead to and be stagnation for your "I am..." in the present. An experidigm that was once joyful and helpful may no longer be helpful, and a new experidigm is needed. If you find your 'I am...' will facing illness, fear, or lack, a new wholeness "I am..." experidigm needs to be created. Visualize it, connect with it, and evolve to the new wholeness experidigm. Keep evolving and making a new experidigm until you acknowledge and receive full wholeness again.

Performing Visual Treatments

Whether you are in a dark room, or you have stopped your path to your NEXT "I am...." experidigm, you need to get going and create your NEXT visualization of your "I am...." life. Your wholeness health depends on the NEXT. Get going. Take a deep breath. Exhale slowly. Take another deep breath. Exhale slowly. Ok, you are stress free and centered again. Now go out and get yourself in a positon to choose new experiences and connect.

WARNING. Let me share my greatest experience in life. Saying it in your mind does not just make it happen. Nor will your words ever fully describe what you see in your mind's eye as your "I am...." connected NEXT experidigm. You have to really work at visualizing what that NEXT is and how to share that NEXT with other "I am...s." Words are ALWAYS misinterpreted by others, and they put your words in their context and not yours!!! Your NEXT will be misinterpreted by everyone. You must visualize it, revisualize it, and keep evolving it until other "I am...s" can participate and share with you. This is the most frustrating process of your experidigm creation. It is so clear to you, so why can others not see it? Because they are not the unique you. You must keep adding more and more detail to your experidigm and grow into it. By sharing it, the questions others ask shed more light as to what your experidigm is.

You get what you ask for. If what you ask for is confusing and vague, you get confusing and vague. This may lead to more frustration with expectations not being met. The reason expectations are not met is you were not able to express the wholeness of your experidigm. Many religions and spiritual practices suggest that you treat or pray or ask for what you need. This is good, but if you just use words, you could be setting yourself up for frustration and this frustration could lead down the path of "you are...." Get your expectations in line and keep drawing a picture of your experidigm, and keep sharing. See how to visualize and make choices in my book *Choosing Up*.

CAUTION. I have talked in the past about the poor descriptive power of words. Words carry a made up duality with them, and this duality does not exist in your "I am...," but it does exist in "you are...." Using words to picture your future and describe your future puts you squarely in the 'You are...' world of being defined in terms of the "you are...." world. Stay away from the "you are...." world when you are visualizing and communicating your wholeness experidigm.

Ok, you want abundance, and you want to escape the lack in your life. You want out of the dark, bare room. Repeating over and over in your mind and to your connected people that you want "money" or "wealth" is just not going to be enough personal information to make the request operational to the infinite connection. Make your vision far more operational for this space suit; picture doing what makes you "wealthy" and share this. This could be a picture of you riding your bike with your family, or working and smiling as you read your paycheck, or eating a great meal with your friends. Pick one to start with and go to it and add more to go to NEXT.

There are an infinite number of "wealth" experidigms, and just saying the "word" and asking for the word confuses your expectations and all who you share with it. Picture, start doing, start sharing, and start evolving.

Ok, sometimes words may appear to be simple enough, but they only deliver simply. "I want to be a lawyer". But, it turns out you actually became a divorce lawyer, and not the intellectual property lawyer you were thinking about. You did not fully visualize and share. Another example is to pray and treat for abundance, and just use the word "money", and that is what is expected to be received. The potential receiver visualizes a $100 bill because they never have seen a higher bill than that. So, one waits for and expects the $100 bill. The bill does not come. The treatment for $100 is shared with my "I am..." friends and I know they understand, but they are not connecting with me because my $100 is not coming. Others tell me to be more specific and use different words, but I get the same result -- nothing. I know this seems trivial, but this is what normally occurs. Our words are just too abstract, to non-visual, to non-action based to actually be sharing a vision of what we want, what our experidigm really is, and know how to act for it.

The reality is that another "I am..." must act on your prayer or treatment statement, and if it is too abstract, too wordy, the reaction one receives might be much different than that which was expected. To improve this lack of clarity, use visual experidigms, prayers and treatments and keep adding to those visual pictures, making them a full experidigm with visuals, words, actions, context, integrations and connections. This is your experidigm "I am…" experidigm prayer and treatment.

The more one communicates and connects the visual experidigm prayer and treatment, the more the creative "I am..." can act in the right direction for the experidigm. The communication and connection must overcome the mass delusion that is being communicated in the background behind one's experidigm. Keep sharing the "I am..." experidigm. In Part 6 the concept of a visual flag for the experidigm will help other "I am...s" rally around the vision. Make the experidigm prayer public, not private.

Our space suits connect us to the world, so use the space suit to be public. Some feel being private protects them from being hurt by the TTers and Takers. The reality is one needs to deflect the TTers and live publicly in the world sharing and connecting.

Healing is seeing the whole and ensuring the whole. Healing a part is only a part. The focus on the whole and how the whole best operates is the focus of an experidigm focused on health. Call such an experidigm focused on whole health an "experihealth" to signify the whole space suit and the "I am…" are healed together.

No Walls Needed

We have talked about healing from your practical ability to visualize the future and attract that future, no matter what your senses say or what the physical world looks like it is manifesting. The ailments of the world are just a manifestation of what the world is thinking. Unfortunately, as we have talked earlier (*Avoid Takers* book as well), individuals, groups, and the media in the world create problems to solve, and they market these problems for others to solve. This brings you into the Taker cycle and a person can easily lose their "I am…." and buy into the problem delusion.

A common delusional problem created by people and groups is the need to protect or defend one's group or oneself because the "different" others will cause hurt, harm or death. This cry of protection is nothing more than a Taker creating a problem and enlisting individuals and entire nations to defend against the different people (and in extreme cases attack and totally kill all different people). Let's build a wall or create an army to defend ourselves. The energy and resources from good meaning people go to support such a bad idea. This bad idea begins to dominate thinking and acting and creates a "you are...." in everyone involved.

The reality of any bad idea is that it dies. No bad idea lives for long. In addition, those supporting bad ideas disappear when the ideas disappear. Hopefully, they go on to good ideas. Living a life in protection or defensive mode, or building a wall around oneself are always bad ideas. Bad ideas destroy themselves. Destructive ideas self-destruct.

Healing will not occur if individuals build a wall around themselves for protection and defense. The wall will keep out the infinite good that will do the healing. A wall assumes you have made a judgment about the "bad-ness" of something. It is far better to respect life and show this respect with discernment and your "I am...." will. Base your judgments first on respect and love, and express your "I am...." instead of building a wall. Do no harm. You never need to accept the Taker problems. Use your "I am...." will to articulate the issues with the Taker problem - this is a far more productive good idea than the bad idea of building a wall from fear of being different.

Good ideas tend to encourage connections and experidigms, leading to joy. Good ideas attract more good ideas. Walls (i.e. fear, defensiveness, and protectionism) stop ideas. Once you build a wall, you become uncon-nected, and the only way for the unconnected to have anything is to take from the connected.

Just as joy is a spiritual state of mind, so is security. No wall will really give security. Security comes from expressing the "I am...."

The defensive and protection fear is imaginary. The fear, and fear is a cre-ated imagery nightmare, is a really bad idea. The nightmare appears tem-porarily true to all who belief in it, until......until the bad idea nightmare dies, and it will die. Hopefully, those with the nightmare wake up before they suffer the fate of their nightmare, but only they know, because it is their nightmare. Get away from Takers and their nightmares.

Building a wall in your mind will stop your healing.

After reading this, you might be thinking "the world is a dangerous place" such that I need to protect and defend myself from dangerous and evil people. Just listen to yourself. You have bought the problem and the delusion, and you are subject to the whims of the Taker! Your mind is being dominated by their Taker delusional problem, and your actions and thoughts are being manipulated and spent on a Taker problem. You have forgot your "I am...." will. You give strength to bad ideas and keep them alive. Bad ideas die.

Why does this bad idea of a "wall" repeat itself through history? Because fear is the easiest tool for a Taker to use to create an imaginary, nightmare problem. Use fear to say that the difference the others have is dangerous, then, now, we need to ...destroy them or separate them or wall them... what comes from bad ideas if acted upon are bad actions. The Taker smiles. In history, those who have tried to build walls or destroy their apparently different neighbors have ended up destroying themselves. A modern day example is the Berlin wall in Germany created after World War II to separate east versus west political ideologies. Ancient history has examples like the fall of Troy or the fall of Jerusalem to the Romans.

One of the most common human wall building delusions of TTers and Takers is to create false experidigms where the future is defined on the basis of "you are..." accusations against different countries or societies. Each side paints the other side as evil, many times using religious terms and how God is on their own side and against the other side. Just a few examples include Irish Catholics versus Protestants, Israel versus the Palestinians, European pioneers vs Native Americans, communism versus democracy, Hitler vs Jews. This list, unfortunately, can be longer than this entire book. When a "you are... defines another group as evil, the end result is the destruction of both sides. Realize that both sides have defined themselves as "you are..." and can only take, not create. They take until they destroy all. Some "I am..." will survive to create and rebuild the "I am..." connected world. Any "you are…" is destructive and taking. "You are…" always judges in such a way to put themselves as superior to take, and if they are not successful at first, the taking will rise to levels until taking or death occurs. Why is this? Takers can only take, not create or connect. In the extreme, Takers risk all to survive by taking. There are no limits to what a Taker will take.

Takers do not care if they destroy you. The only answer to a wall is "I am…." connected and experiencing.

Flow of Joy

Joy is not stagnant. Joy will not exist in a stagnant life. Joy flows from actively connecting and experiencing. Connections and experiences are always flowing to a new joy, refreshing joy, and not necessarily more joy as additive, but a bit more complex, more fully alive and with a broader perspective. Sometimes redoing an "old" experience in a new context is better than, and more unique, than the old joy you experienced.

There is an infinite number of flows and an infinite number of contexts. Each context and time is different, which allows simple changes to current experience to see joy in the NEXT experience. The same flow in different contexts will give entirely different experiences.

Here is a simple drawing that shows how to visualize a sample of joy flows and how they are related to refreshes and connections:

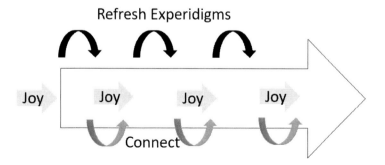

Joy will always continue to flow. The question is whether you will want to be in the joy flow. Unfortunately, sometimes people use their "I am..." connections and experiences to get what they want and need, like a new job, and once one has that new thing, one might covet it and slip where one wants to keep that feeling and not change and keep life "as is". This leads to falling into stagnation and the delusion one can hold onto this stagnation while the world changes and flows all around. The very "I am..." used to get the new thing, is later trapped behind a "you are..." status quo façade. Connections are so important to warn the now "you are..." that they have slipped and are in danger of being disconnected from the joy flow. Getting back to the "I am..." flow might take significant time, depending on how much you hurt others with your "you are..." statements and actions.

PART 5:
Rules of Experidigm Economy

Witness Experidigm Economy

With the goal in life to be joyous by creating experiences and connections, it would be good to have the resources to pursue your experidigms. It would also be good to have all your connections have the resources to pursue their experiences and connections. Some resources can be common and shared and assist all people, like learning and education, communication, travel, food, etc. The goal is for each person to keep moving to more and more experidigms. Everyone is creating, growing, and innovating. Very much value and wealth should be created. The economic Theory of the Experidigm is that excess wealth should be invested back to the larger group involved in creating that experidigm and to create group Joy infrastructure for the future. Perhaps the excess profits are so large the profits can create an experidigm infrastructure where all the suppliers and manufacturers join with all the customers to create a growing and evolving experidigm community. Is this what the online businesses that have hundreds of millions of users evolve toward and become?

The last one hundred years have seen tremendous productivity advances from efficiency, effectiveness, automation, and machine intelligence.

Human beings are being designed out of the manufacturing, shipping, and service processes. In another fifty or so years, artificial intelligence, robot apps, and an even more advanced internet will not really require many people to work, except to buy things. Excess profits will continue to flow to fewer and fewer owners. The "invisible hand" of the market no longer is invisible. It is crystal clear what ownership hands dominant each market in the world. As population growth naturally occurs, and as business owner hands reduce the need for workers, the profits in excess will grow even faster.

If profits in excess are used to enable an experidigm community, then "I am…s" must shine much brighter. Excess resources should focus on the Joy equation and enabling resources for experidigms and connections while retraining "you are…s" to be creative "I am…s." Part 7 talks about education required. Can society change how value is shared?

Obviously, one of the greatest questions in any economy is how do we reward the labor of each individual and how do we deal with the excess profits/resources that that labor creates? With a goal to increase the potential joy of all participants in the end, it is up to individuals to freely choose what labor they do. Who is in charge of getting the profits and what should be done with those profits? Why can profits be horded by a few? The goal in life should not be to horde money.

The reality is most societies have created a dominate "you are…" worker world and a "you are…" owner world, and the societies have defined and accepted these "you are…" roles and let the few "owners" have the profits of the labors of all others, as long as the owner retains ownership (no matter what was originally required to be called owner). Is this still a good model when the profits can be logarithmically higher than any other participants share? We now live in a world where a few "owners" dominate the created wealth of all others. We will address later this massive excess in profits in relation to the Joy equation. How did this disconnect between "excess created" value (notion of reward for risk?) and reward happen, and continues to happen in history? More efficient production and distribution systems along with greed allow the collection of wealth. Nature does not accumulate wealth. Nature uses what it needs now and cooperates to deliver what it needs now.

I am not implying that capitalism or that any economic system generating profits is bad. Nor am I suggesting a socialistic type of society is good. I am suggesting that excess value is related to the efforts of those in the experidigm, and the value should flow to those based on that effort, including owners, employees, customers, and the society that is impacted and supports the experidigm. The excess should not be the exclusive property of the owners. The experidigm participants should participate in sharing the excess profits. Currently, excess profits flow to only a small fraction of people creating the experidigm wealth. New methods of enabling the experidigm with excess profits are needed.

The word excess means payments beyond reasonable salaries and a simple return on capital invested. This salary and investment world is a remnant of our manufacturing and product based industrialized world. What happens if our world is evolving from selling products to selling experiences? This has a dramatic impact on how "excess profits are distributed as we see through the remainder of this Part and the next Part.

More disappointing about historical economies, and what many workers and owners struggle with, is trying to support their "I am..." with "I am..." type of work in a dominant "you are..." work world. Does working in a "you are..." work world and being subject to the constant demands of the "you are..." status-quo keepers encouraging you to "fit in," damage the "I am...?" Workers flip an internal switch and protect their 'I am...' while at work, and then flip the switch back when they leave work – hopefully they are able to do that and not get stuck with the "I am..." switch off. Have we reached a point in history where work can add to our 'I am...' by creating experiences for us and more connections? Perhaps, but that would require that a work goal would be joy, not just profits. The belief that profits and wages are being invested wisely to create personal joy, might be an unconnected "you are..."type of thinking. What kind of sense does it make to live and work in someone else's 'You are...'" delusion, especially if they take all excess profits and keep them for their own joy. This does not make sense to the "I am...," so why does it happen? It happens because we live in a "you are..." thinking world at work.

This parts and product world assumes consumers can select and integrate all the selections into a holistic life experience that is joyful. This parts view assumes everyone knows how to install and maintain each component they purchase and integrate it with all other products one has. Our product manufacturing and distribution supply chains have become so efficient and effective we get good low cost, quality products. The economy is very good at making and moving, but we are not nearly as efficient at effectively using, refreshing and disposing of products. The average person probably uses each product at very low efficiency as compared to how it was designed. I have been using spreadsheets and presentation software for 20 plus years and only scratch the surface of the software's capabilities. Try not changing the oil in a car for 70,000 miles and see what happens to the efficiency of the car. Products can be used in non-perfect ways. Many products together can be used in many non-perfect ways. All the parts we have do not add up to very much if we have not envisioned an experidigm and enlisted a good group of connections to help us make the right selections and integrations. We are rapidly moving to the experience economy where the connections ensure that the parts have been effectively integrated into a joyful holistic experience.

In the buying experience future, a major technology skill is to be a designer of certain types of experiences and advise others how to assemble and do that experience in a joyful way for all today and for future generations.

Equal Value

In my book *Avoiding Takers* I talk about equal value sharing with trades and how individual incentives will be changing in the transition from the product world to the experidigm world.

Equal Sharer Trade

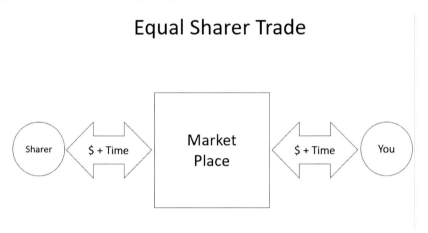

Key to thoughts on value is how we currently put a value on physical products by giving them a price. We live in a product world now where we manufacture, sell and buy products. That product world will continue to exist, just like an agricultural world exists in an industrial world. The product world will evolve into a multi-experience world. We will have an agricultural world, an industrial world, a product world, and an experidigm world at the same time.

In the material product world, joy comes from the use of the products. In the experience world, joy comes from having the entire creative experience. This experience world puts a premium on creativity around an experience to fit an "I am...."

Products are fleeting in the service of delivering the experience. Connections that assist with the experience become more important. Products are the result of choices to get your experience. Like products, possessions are also in the service of the experience. Possession and products can act as an infrastructure to support our experiences. This support can be composed of both public and private infrastructures. Value can support both public and private interests, and this is why excess value is important, because it can build both public and private infrastructures. A public infrastructure can enhance all individual joy. Excess value has no value to society if it cannot be used to build more public joy. A goal is to have more choice for all levels of society and to have the ability to form more connections in society. As an example, connections in society have been enhanced by building public roads, public communication networks (i.e. internet and phones), public schools, etc. More choice happens by having more educated people and by restricting "You are..." people with moral laws to protect freedom and private rights. Excess profits can be invested back in to the entire experidigm community that created both the excess profit and the joyful experidigm.

The experidigm economy is focused on evolving experiences and creating fresh joy. The product economy is focused on consumption. The product economy assumes that life is simple enough to just consume and not have to think too much about integrating products and choices into our lives. Integrating many products and choices into our lives is no longer trivial and requires design support. To reach for more integration and more experiences, more support of individuals is needed. The experidigm economy is the rise of that expert support to assist in the creation of the connected "I am..." life. Here are some comparisons between a product world and an experience world:

Product vs Experience

+ buy and use vs integrated, holistic experience

+ me alone vs individual plus experts and sharers

+ consume vs grow, expand, smile

+ ads for one vs multiple choice

+	features	vs	how characteristics fit in the whole
+	now	vs	now and future, evolving connected
+	It is mine	vs	group practice and my part
+	assemble	vs	integrate
+	no expertise	vs	sharers and fulfillers needed
+	logistics	vs	marshalling
+	services	vs	growth and spirituality
+	one time	vs	evolve together
+	independent	vs	cooperative
+	use	vs	fulfillment and joy

Grow and Share Together

Laws make sure that individuals are free to work and grow together. We trade and share equal value in an open economy. To share means to trade equal value using open dialogue, not to give away value for free or to have a Taker take the value in a very unequal trade. Sharers have respect for value created, and so sharers expend the resources to create value. They expend resources to tell others about the value and to sell the value. The beauty of sharing is that new knowledge and variety have been created. So much value has been created and accumulated in history, that today we have a much easier time with selecting our many choices for our experidigms. As time goes by, more options for choices are always created. In addition, groups make inventories of experiences that can be shared and added to, always helping to reach the NEXT level of experidigm. Each generation starts with a larger foundation, more ability to connect "I am…s."

You may find yourself in a difficult spot. No one is willing to share with you and to assist you with anything you are doing. "You are..." people surround you. So what do you do? You do three simple steps: 1) you visualize your pointing after experidigm, 2) you ask for specific "expert" help where you think you need it, 3) you keep asking until someone contributes. When someone contributes: 1) you reward them, 2) explain more of your experidigm, and 3) you include them on your experidigm team. And away you stumble to your first experidigm.

Respect & No Underestimation

In a "you are..." world, the judgment of a "you are..." person carries no respect and dramatically underestimates other people. The 'you are...' statement contains the intent to disrespect the "I am..." and then to give a low value to the "I am...." Trying to create the delusion of lower value is the hallmark of a 'you are...' Taker. If a "you are..." can get you to believe you are worthless, they get your creativity and value at low cost. If they can do this to many people, they can create excess profit for themselves. The more they underestimate your value and the more you accept it, the more they make, and they can invest further in keeping the delusion going. In a product-based economy where many people work in the production plant or in the service supply chain, they are removed from the customer, and must listen to the "manager" between them and the customer. If this manager is a Taker, they will be undervalued, and excess profits will be created. In many of these situations, if you reached out to the customer, you will be reprimanded, or, in worst case, you will be fired. The Taker does not want the delusion shattered by your relating to the customer.

An experidigmer economy is not a product economy or a supplier economy. It is an experience economy and those that participate in the experience with the customer will share their value. In a very real direct way, they are either part of the experience, or not. Big data does not connect them or drive the relationship, but big data does make any product movement efficient and low cost. What drives the relationship is direct communication of expertise and connection to the exact context (work, play, travel, or whatever action experience) of the experidigmer. The many actions required by the user will be linked to their "expert" to make sure the context of the action is related to the desires and joy of the experidigmer.

If lack of respect or being undervalued is shown by any party in the experience, the other party must reevaluate the relationship, because the "you are…" is direct and known. The connectivity allows them to find other participants. In an experidigm economy, undervaluing does occur; it is direct, and it is not managed by an independent manager (like in the product manager world) in the manager's best interest instead of the worker and the customer. I know this sounds idealistic, but whenever a worker is not directly related to a customer, the workers value will be manipulated against them by the intermediary. Most relationships in the experience economy will be directly managed by the participants and their "I am…" connections.

That is the power of the new connectivity with your experidigmer team of experts. Products are secondary – it is the relationship that counts, and how that relationship creates more joyful experiences. Just as the industrial revolution and automation shifted labor from agriculture to the product factory, the connected world will shift labor from a product world to an experience world where the vast majority of people will be directly related to customers because of some actions required of the customer.

Action & Experience Expertise

Action in context to the experidigm is the key to the experidigm economy. Action can be designed by the experidigmers with their connected group of "experts" defining what those actions are is crucial for each experience. Since each experience always evolves and is not perfect in its inspiration, the connection to a team must always be made to enhance the actions. The team is not static and will evolve as the value supplied is understood and leads to more joy. Joy is what happens when action is carried out from an "I am..." vision. Here is a sample action strip for a simple day first shown in *Soaring to Awesome*:

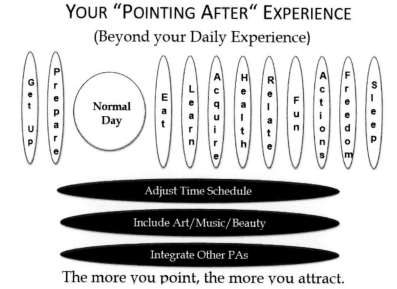

YOUR "POINTING AFTER" EXPERIENCE
(Beyond your Daily Experience)

Get Up · Prepare · Normal Day · Eat · Learn · Acquire · Health · Relate · Faith · Fun · Actions · Freedom · Sleep

Adjust Time Schedule

Include Art/Music/Beauty

Integrate Other PAs

The more you point, the more you attract.

This is like in the old "craft" world (local farmer, local blacksmith/welder, local veterinarian, etc.) where experts managed their trade and shared their expertise to increase the experiences of those with whom they interacted -- it required direct contact. In the experidigm world, we live with a product saturated world where the knowledge of how to combine things and experience these things together in the context we want is most important, but not yet fully understood. Already, in many products, we use far fewer features and capabilities of the product because we just do not have the action understanding how to use products to their full individual or combined capability. Product suppliers might not know our surrounding experience, so they are ill-equipped to help. A working group of expert action craft people will create and support the experience economy and connect their actions through an online communication connection as described in *Choosing Up*.

Measuring Success vs Target

How do you measure success of an experience? Broadly smiling is a good start and wanting to improve the experience is another. The best way to measure success is to compare the activity you do to the one you had visualized and mapped out. This is really simple. Experidigmers set a specific holistic target for every experience and measure the key attributes they want, and compares these attributes to what actually happens. If your experience is health, one can set targets for exercise, body metabolism (i.e. blood pressure), eating habits, and sleeping habits. We check how we are doing versus targets and make changes to better move forward to our experidigm.

Companies do this every day and set up at least monthly reviews to see how they are doing versus target. Companies compare their budgets (i.e. targets) versus the actual results for sales, costs, profits, inventory, manpower, etc. Customers also measure their success versus target. In the product world, customers can look at product feature performance versus claimed, and relate this to how much they paid. Did customers get the value they wanted for the product? If something does not match the target in the product world, customers do not buy that product again and go to a competitor.

In the experience economy, customers must look at the value each connection and each product and each service gives to their experidigm. In the experience economy, since the experidigm is known, and the design is visualized and published, those selling products must be involved with how the customer integrates their product into the experidigm and customers will measure how it works with their experience. Experts can advise how well each product may fit into the experidigm. As described in *Choosing Up*, the experidigmer can have online meetings with their connected team and review how well they are doing with moving toward the experidigm and how each recommendation from experts is doing.

Given how easy and low cost it is to install sensors and link these sensors to software that compares what is being sensed to target, the experidigmer can make real time adjustments. For example, in comparing our health to better health targets, sensed data can immediately help decide what to eat versus target. A resting target blood pressure of 120/80 is the target, but the blood pressure is seen rising to 140/90 and going higher. This might be caused by the caffeine consumed, or to stress. Now we are alerted, so we eat some garlic and turmeric to lower the pressure.

Always moving forward to the pointing up experidigm is very important to prevent stagnation or addiction. If progress is not measured versus target, is progress really being made? Daily measurements may indicate we are making progress, but we maybe just stuck in place and making ourselves feel good. Days, months and years go by and really nothing happened versus target. At work this happens when the daily routine is filled with task after task that gives the delusion progress is being made upward, but remain in the same job, just doing the same tasks in a different order and not progressing at all. Keeping busy is not making progress. At home, wanting to lose weight, and looking in the mirror each morning at the stomach and saying, "looking better" when stepping on a scale every day at the same time would tell a different story of no change, and in fact, a slight gain. I did this and stayed the same weight for three years – I had convinced myself I was doing well. Feeling good is not necessarily making progress. The best way to overcome this is to compare progress versus the current experidigm, using the Oudit approach. The Oudit approach is the act of comparing your actual experidigm experience to the original visual experidigm, noting any differences, and changing actions to achieve the original experidigm or creating a new experidigm. The Oudit process could include actual sensed measurements, like measuring heart rate and blood pressure when performing a health experidigm.

Keep the experidigm picture in front of you, pointing upward, and make decisions and selections each day toward the experidigm. The first level of adjustment is to check if you make decisions and selections each day moving however slowly and upwardly to the experidigm. Just write down the decisions and selections you made every day and check them every few weeks. Make sure you go to NEXT at least every year or so. The second level of adjustment from comparing to target is to discuss "issues" and NEXTs with connections and listen to connections about your progress and then suggest adjustments. The third level is to set up sign posts (like warnings or alarms) to automatically alert for progress. These alerts can come as a result of real time sensed data compared to target, and the level versus target is unacceptable, so a warning would be sent.

New Components List

In the new economy, the current things done now will continue, but they will not be the focus; instead they will just be an option. The focus will be on the whole experience so joy can be enhanced. In this list below, the first item mentioned is the new focus, and the second "vs" item is the way now.

+ Joy is focus...price vs Joy

+ Experience is the new product… experience multi-choice vs 1 product feature

+ Connections, not big data, expand choice and knowledge in service of the experience… better communications to share actions vs figure it out alone

+ Experts vs product collateral

+ Action strips vs supply chain efficiency

+ Big data decision models assist in individual decision making and comparison to best for each experidigmer (i.e. Oudit target comparisons in later Part) vs haphazard

+ Experience property versus private property

+ Experience platform (not just building roads for cars, but connectivity for all) vs excess profit

+ Experience expertise vs capital for plants/property

+ Hand up vs hand out

The experience economy builds on the past focus and expands.

Current Law Impact

To make the transition painlessly to an experidigm economy will not occur smoothly for many, especially those in 100% product industries as they lose excess profits to the experidigm economy. Current laws are set up to protect what already exists and preserve that from changes. The type of laws that will slow transition the most are "tax" laws, as local, state and federal government try to keep the tax money coming in to support their spending.

Taxes are easy to identify when a product or service is sold, and when identified a sales tax is levied and collected. In the end, the customer pays the product sales tax as the supplier just passes it through to the consumer. These types of taxes can be in many different forms, like hotels paying city and state fees for each overnight stay, or taxicabs paying the city a medallion fee to get the right to be a taxicab.

The transaction is not that clear in the Experidigm economy, and who should be taxed and when and how is the tax applied might be highly variable. The transaction is trading different kinds of value and joy and, in the short term, the value sent both ways is not easily measured if money does not change hands. Governments are just not set up to deal with this change while still in the product economy. Product companies are fine with the status quo of taxation and want any new competitor to pay similar taxes or more. Product companies will lobby governments to tax the Experidigm economy companies trading in experience and action expertise. In the short term, the product companies will be successful in slowing down the experience economy by adding prohibitive taxation, but this will not last as the experience economy spreads because of the vast ability to connect and build experidigms together.

Another issue that governments may struggle with is how the services they supply will be measured and compared to the agreed upon target of service. The collection of data showing how well governments did versus target could be in the open public domain, no longer just subject to individual experience with the related beliefs and the political process—it will be made real and understandable to all. Governments can be held accountable for the experiences they deliver and questioned whether they should be delivering these experiences or some other experience organization.

In an experidigmer joy and connected economy, the role of government may shift from a mentality of a "hand-out" role to the less fortunate to a "hand-up" role involving the less fortunate in experiences. In a connected world, involving people in connections will be very important. A by-product of the material product world is that people live so independently with their products, the delusion is that the product brings joy and we do not need many connections if any. If product connections lead us down a "you are..." path, then we just get more and more disconnected. What happened to the extended connections of the family of the local community in a "you are..." world? In a connected experidigmer world, there is no need for a "hand out," only needs for a "hand up". Giving money to the disconnected may feel good to the heart, but it does little to connect and give a hand-up. Give and make connections focused on experidigms.

Current Organization Impact

Most current business product companies and governments are structured in silos to deliver individual products/services. Each silo has its own budget and is expected to compete against other silos to, at least, do as well as other silos with their budget. But, each silo competes for resources, so they are fiercely loyal to their own and fight other silos for their fair share of resources and excess profits. Business silo leaders have titles like general manager, product manager, brand manager, category manager, or functional manager. They manage their kingdoms so they get the rewards. From a silo structure, customers receive products from an efficient supply chain at a "reasonable" cost. If the customer knows how to use this product and fully integrate "I am..." into their experience, this reasonable cost product is good.

What happens if customers cannot understand and integrate this new product into their changing life? Product companies largely do not have a "service" that does integration unless they can sell you more products through the same supply chain (called "cross selling). Cross selling usually still leaves integration in to the bigger experience up to the customers. Each independent silo does not really want to work with other silos to deliver an "integrated" experience to a customer. Remember, silos are in competition with each other. Silos do not trust each other. Obviously, there is an organizational structure issue for product firms to deliver the integrated experidigm.

There are organizational solutions for product firms that want to deliver experidigms (see *Choosing Up*), but the transition will be subject to extreme *Turd Throwers* (see *Soaring to Awesome*).

Instead, organizations built on internet connections with their experts bringing real time discussions directly to customers will have an advantage to deliver experiences in a real time, evolving fashion. (Note: see my book *Choosing Up* that describes this).

Each customized "I am..." experidigm is best delivered when connected over time with a group of experts incentivized to participate. Sure, products will be sold as well as experiences, but the value driving force is the joy of the experience and connections.

Made-Up Stories

Any economy is supported by stories. Picture a sleepy little town in the western USA that suddenly creates a story of "Gold!", and they say "come to our town and strike it rich". Overnight the town grows a 100 fold. You say this does not happen in the modern world? Yes it does. "We make steel, and come and work in our steel mills" – now rust towns. "We have natural gas, come and work on our rigs". This is happening in many towns throughout the world. In each town, the status quo is telling its story and this story will keep the same leaders in power and taking. The town stories have drifted from "passively" reporting the story of the day to creating and telling the made-up story that fits with the singular dream of the status quo. This is neither good nor bad. This is the way it is. Hopefully, the town story is open, inclusive, and growth and joy orientated – if not, it is like a stagnant prison cell.

The good news is that "I am...ers" can tell their story about their current experidigm and what they are evolving to, and that others can join. Instead of a physical location, like a town, to go to and experience your fulfilling life, you create your visual of your future and share that to have people to come and participate with you, regardless of where you are located. The gold rushes of tomorrow will be great experidigms with which to be connected.

Joyful Days

Living in a working life in a product world is not that joyful. Working all day for someone else just to sleep under your own roof in your own bed is really not a joyful experidigm.

The joyful experidigm economy will allow your "I am..." to connect. You will connect with something new:

+ by doing

+ by learning

+ by meeting together and sharing experidigms

+ by choosing several times a day

+ by finding more sharers and building your team

+ by adding to your experidigm

+ by listening

+ by loving

+ by caring

Experidigms focus on action and joy.

PART 6:

Path of Life

The Path

Everyone has a Path of Life, or many paths. It is not just a work career. The Path does not have a goal at the end. It is not a "you are..." designated project list of accomplishments and success. The Path has to do with your joy. It is your playground that changes every day, for you to create and recreate. It is your "I am..." continuous journey of joy. Your experiences keep the joy fresh. It is your connections that assist you and share all kinds of joy.

The Path has no destination. You will never arrive and be done. You will always be "I am...." "I am..." already has access to all the infinite. How you experience and connect is the joy of the Path. The Path is here now for your attention in this space suit. You choose your path and your experidigms. Yes, you choose with the assistance and guidance of the Infinite "I am..." and other "I am...s." The gift of "I am..." is given, so use it. Keep creating. Be aware and recognize this is your "I am..." path, and not anyone else's past, present, or future. It is your gift to receive and share. Welcome to your Path! Let go of all your limiting notions and start your unlimited Path. Life is not for just living, but growing, and evolving up your Path to your visual pointing afters. Fast or slow progress makes no difference. It is your pace, and since there is no destination, you will get there over and over again, so enjoy the Path. You will stand out, and you will stand out again and again. Bad people will focus on you, to constrain you, to cut you down to their size, but they are not on your Path. They are a deterrent to your movement and flow. Invite in only those who enable your flow.

Start small. Keep it small if you like, but keep pointing up and flowing.

The Path of Life above shows to break free of Takers and *Avoid Takers* and then work with your team to visualize your experidigm (both *Elements of Visual Talking* and *Choosing Up* are helpful). But, TTers will see you are breaking free from the status quo and will try to stop you. By using your TTer deflection shield described in *Soaring to Awesome – Turd Throwers Beware*, you will be able to climb over their blocking wall to your experidigm and many more experidigms. Once free from TTers, you will be able to connect and share with all "I am…s."

Lead Your Parade

Only your "I am..." connection knows where your "I am..." is going, so you must share that and lead that. The very good news is that all "I am...s" are connected as a family and can openly share the love carried on the "I am..." connection wave. Together, 'I am...s' share creativity and experidigm possibilities and progress in the infinite. The infinite fiber is joy and love. Your space suit can show the unique joy and love experience at any given time. Your joy and love will keep changing and evolving. In this image I show the constant evolution of your joyful "I am..." as you request NEXT from the Infinite. Your joy evolves.

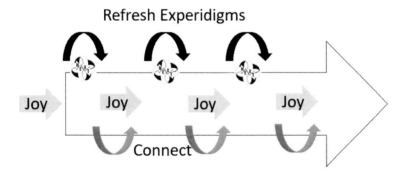

Picture yourself leading your parade through the city. As the march progresses through the city your group of supporters and followers grows and grows. As you lead the parade, you have your flag held high for all to see, and your flag has your experidigm picture on it.

Lead your parade of connections as often as you can. Each time you lead your experience grows. The picture above shows how you point up to your experidigm and use the recommendations and support of your connections.

Shine Outward – Love

The "I am…" power comes from within, through the Infinite "I am… connection" and further expressed with other "I am…" support. No one is alone. All creativity flows from the "I am…" and through the "I am…" to the external world. In the external world, "I am…" experiences flow as the shining out focuses on a shared and connected experidigm. This is not self-discovery per se, nor is it oneness with nature, but more like creativity flowing with loving "I am...ness" from the inside. Focus and pointing to the full experidigm drives action. Sadness, melancholy, loneliness, and raw negativity appear when focus and pointing are lost and the "you are..." world is taking from the "I am...." Our joy shines out of the "I am...." Love carries the shining out to other "I am...s," and connection happens.

What does it feel like when not shining out? The feeling is disconnected and horrible, like a part of being is lost. One is left feeling susceptible, alone, and searching to join something. Do not settle for joining the status quo and staying stagnant. Have patience. The individual "I am..." will shine again. Love is always flowing around us. Love never stops. Similar to love is lightness – you know lightness exists no matter where you are and what you are doing. Love exists the same way. Smile, and shine outward to meet love in the flow. Just say NEXT, and get in the flow and the limitlessness of your "I am...."

Love is connecting and doing experidigms together.

A Day in the Life

This picture shows how all of the components come together to create a great day. The components are shared by your connections. This is an example from *Choosing Up*:

You might think that doing this every day is a bit much, and you need some consistency and constancy. You do need some consistency and constancy -- and that is what you get with your "I am..." connection! It is the "you are..." unconnected challenges you need to escape from every day and just eliminate them from your life permanently. Without "you are..." in your life, joy and love wash over you as a never ending soothing wave.

Here is a checklist to help you experience joy every day:

Accomplish in Order	Check
Declare "I am..." using Free Will	
Visualize two example experidigms	
at play	
at work	
Pick helpful and expert teams	
at play	
at work	
Select choices for each experidigm	
Compare choice results with target	
Evolve to NEXT	

Since a major component of the Joy equation is to connect, here are ways to connect and share every day:

+ Smile at those around you

+ Witness the supernatural

+ Pray...

+ Hear and share

+ Do quick updates

+ Directly connect and share and touch...

Another way to have a great day is to go to places again, but since the timing is different, so is the experidigm:

+ where you feel all the participation and the first emotions of discovery.

+ Such joy at looking at the past anew...the past always feels better than it might have been...adding to a past pointing after experidigm is wonderful

Renew and grow.

Challenges

Even with perfect experidigms, at times challenges will need to be overcome. Some challenges to be aware of and manage are drifting from connections, negatively judging others, fear, and an excuses mindset.

+ Drifting from Connections:

As we get involved in our life, our focus can take us down a narrow path. That is ok and required many times to reach individual joy. But, we must keep in mind our connections, our family, and our experts and share with them our lives and listen to them so they can share their lives with us. We must share our lives and experidigms, or we can lose connections. Connections are so hard to build back up.

How does this happen? Connecting is a two-way street and requires information, care, and loving flow both ways. When the flow both ways gets out of balance, misunderstanding creeps in and causes problems. Not only are expert connections giving advice, they are receiving updates on how the situation changes and on how their advice impacts that. A common problem is drifting apart and not updating each other on changes, progress, or improvements. Here is a sample dialogue:

"How are you? We have not talked in a while."

"You do not call or care. I have serious issues with you...."

"I am sorry and hope all is better."

"You just do not care!"

"I care greatly, but I cannot read your mind. You need to tell me what is going on with you."

The bottom line is these two people stopped talking and then blame each other for that. Because of that, they stopped their relationship and their sharing. This happens a lot when connections do not update each other. Please do your part and share your experidigm in a positive, non-bragging way with no expectations for a response needed.

Another connection problem is to keep asking and receiving and not giving. Connections will drop out if they are not rewarded and thanked. Keep connecting.

Over-connecting is OK. Just make sure both sides of the connection are benefitting and working on their respective experidigm. Setting up meeting times will help align expectations and help everyone to plan for discussions and meetings. Everyone can meaningfully contribute and participate.

The back book cover for *Choosing Up* has a picture of an experidigmer pointing to their experidigm and standing on the expert wisdom of his connected experidigm team, connected online from anywhere. See in the picture below how all of the connected team are supporting and looking at the experidigm and making changes to it, so all see the changes and suggestions. Using online connection groupware software or social media sites can be very helpful to connect across geographic barriers and across time zones.

Building an experidigm is not a solo effort. Leverage the ideas and experience of those who participate in your parade. Any miscommunication can be corrected by honest dialogue.

This is the crazy thing about connections -- they expect us to read their minds. When we do not do so correctly, they assume the worst. They assume we do not care. Once feelings get hurt, they stay hurt if sharing does not occur. This can last a lifetime.

Sharing and connecting is not easy. We must remain diligent and share as often as possible. Just saying "HI" and thanks keep the sharing gate open.

In this easy-to-connect-world online, it appears harder than ever to connect and share time. Just do it often.

+   Judging Others

The world wants us to get involved. When we get involved, we must use discernment to make our choices, evolve our experidigms and live our "I am...." Basically, we only know our 'I am...' and can share our "I am..." and improve our "I am..." That is getting involved in life. When we use our discernment and use it to speak and then say negative "you are..." statements, we have crossed over into speaking out of negative and manipulative judgment. This is a very slippery slope. Speaking "you are..." judgments disconnects us from our "I am...." Frankly, we never fully know someone else's "I am..." so we are not an authority on defining them, and if we think we are, we have slipped away from our "I am..." Do not slip away from your "I am...."

It might feel like you have power and control when you say "you are..." judgments, but the exact opposite happens to you. You just buried your own "I am..." and you are attempting to bury the "I am..." of someone else. Speaking your "you are…" judgments will never increase your connections or joy. You are on the slippery slope to becoming a disconnected "you are..." turd thrower.

+   Overcoming Fear Judgments

The only authority in life is the connection to the Infinite, and anything that challenges that connection is a "You are." delusion. Love and trust are imbedded in the "I am..." connection and are the "I am..." connection. Love and trust can be defined as feelings or such, but that puts them squarely in the space suit sensing and a "you are..." judgment world. Love and trust are part of your "I am..." connection, but without a connection, love and trust are only temporary physical space suit things.

Love and trust exist only in sharing a connection of "I am..." and witnessing each other in the act of creating positivity through the Infinite – when you express joy in the creation journey to Pointing After (PA) experidigm. Fear is a space suit feeling in the unconnected realm and is a delusion that can disconnect the Infinite, love and trust.

And, giving is not sharing. Giving is a one-time act that satisfies a one-time need, while sharing is an on-going connection that ensures "I am...s" are connected. A TTer/Taker can give, but has extreme trouble with sharing. Sometimes giving occurs because of a "you are..." feeling of fear and fearing discipline if do not give – fear of being judged as negative or an evil Grinch.

+   Getting Lost - Excuses

There are many things that will push you down the path of getting lost. All of the reasons may look as if they conspire to make sure you get and stay lost from your "I am...." Some reasons include a "you are..." redefining you and you letting that in and accepting it, or you let fear take you down its' path, or you get addicted to status quo and stop any change thereby getting stuck. No matter what the reason is for getting lost, **it is your personal excuse** to keep you lost.

Excuses keep you exactly where you are. Your mind says them to you, and you accept them. It is that easy. I know you think your reasons are not excuses. You think they are valid facts and justifiable from real observation and experience. You have deluded yourself and allowed yourself to get lost. You carry your excuses around with you to defend yourself for the great future staring back at you. When others point to a better future, you throw your excuses like knives at them. You want to kill them and keep your excuses. Soon, others stop wanting to support your future because you defend and live in your excuses. It is a self-fulfilling prophecy.

Getting lost in excuses is easily broken. First, no excuses. Substitute choice and NEXT for your excuse mentality. Second, create your vision of a pointing after experidigm. Third, make your first choice. You are now back on the Path and others will see your confidence and join you in your journey again. You no longer throw your excuse knives at them.

Growth

Without growth, there is stagnation and the potential addiction to keep one in stagnation. It is easy to stagnant. It is not hard to grow, but it might look that way if you are stagnant. Growth occurs when you move toward something, toward your NEXT experidigm. We learn every time we take a step forward to NEXT. Each NEXT gets us another connection into infinity.

As we discussed earlier, growth spreads through time according to the S-curve, and each experidigm has his own curve so you can grow quicker with a cumulative impact. We can reach out to other growth curves from those with whom we connect. We can share choices in each curve. We can teach others to grow, and in turn, learn from them. Sharing dramatically extends the choices and experidigms we can understand and then choose to select some aspect from the new experidigm of others.

Why is continuous growth so important? Continuous growth always contains creative energy and the ability to build. Growth does not imply simple and same operations but changing operations. To change requires will and creativity. Machines have no will or creativity – machines do not grow. They only operate within their design parameters. To change and grow, a machine requires creativity from an "I am…." Without the growth will and the "I am…" to create, any person can be a stagnant machine. Machines operate on the same operating mode. Change to that risks the machine not operating. People can live in fear of change and operate like a machine, giving up their will and "I am…." Our space suit is a machine, but our will to growth and the connections of the "I am…" make everyone a joyful person.

The bottom line…more experiences and more connections means growth and joy.

Experidigm Wisdom

Life seems to have so many goals and that having some things, like wisdom and money, make life better. Wrong. Life is really easy and the focus of wisdom is simple.

Wisdom is:

Knowing there are many different perspectives and choices

Asking questions to understand.

Visualizing where you want to go

Selecting what makes you joyful.

Knowing when your "I am..." wants to create.

Most important, only the "I am..." connection really matters.

Wisdom is knowing that only the "I am..." connection matters and has meaning in life, so have joy with the "I am...." This wisdom seems to be the summary of *Ecclesiastes* in the Old Testament as told by an old man, maybe King Solomon. Read *Ecclesiastes12*. The conclusion about wisdom is two-fold: 1) everything earthly is meaningless, and 2) connect with the Infinite "I am..." and accept all the gifts while we can in this earthly space suit. For some readers, this conclusion is depressing. Readers make ask, "You mean no matter how much I do and learn and work, it does not matter? Surely, doing good deeds matter?" Wisdom is not about the accumulation of facts, or about mental ability, or about wealth, or about learning lessons. Wisdom is not a state of being. Wisdom is the simple acceptance and support of the "I am..." and participating in the flow of the creative "I am..." with the Joy equation. What we learn and experience has no meaning in and of itself, except being in the joyful flow with the Infinite. Being in the Joyful flow with the Infinite is the only wisdom needed. This is so uplifting. Shine your light out from your "I am…." Know that you create your experidigm with the gifts your "I am…" connects with and brings into your life. Clearly, this is not materialism or acts of the "flesh," but a spirit connection allowing a creative joy connection.

Spiritual Buddha

We are here on earth to have our "I am…" experience in this space suit. Our space suit is temporary. The space suit is equipped with sensors to help one feel what is around them, so feel. Go and experience in the direction of the experidigm. Although the experience may be earth bound, the act of being creative is an "I am..." connected experience. With "I am…" in the heart and pointing toward an evolving experidigm, joy can be felt. We can overthink and assume the creation of an experidigm seems too materialistic non-Godlike. Or we can overthink to become God-like and try to separate ourselves from the world and meditate and deny that our space suits are given to us. We can live a life of an isolated mind and body and deny everything, including our space suits. Does this make sense, and does it help us experience our 'I am…" journey in this world? Seems strange that the Infinite "I am…" put all this around us for us to ignore it and deny it. What if the Infinite sees through our eyes and experiences through our eyes? Then, meditation is not such a great thing for the Infinite to see and feel from us. Using given ability, gifts of creation, love, and connection, the experidigm focuses on the additional gift of joy being felt in the flow of the "I am…" link. Being disconnected in meditation and inaction puts those gifts in addictive stagnation.

Of course the world contains morally devoid bad "you are…" people who will try to hurt you. This does not mean the answer is to deny your gifts because "you are…" people are trying to take them. Instead, the "I am…" must learn to deal with the "you are…" and select the "I am…" that experiences and connects. Avoiding the gifts of the "I am..." and building a life of separation is a life built on fear – fear of the beautiful creativity of the "I am…."

We create and select the way we live our life. Human life is not constrained by the "I am…." Human life is constrained by the poor "you are…" decisions one accepts and makes. If one wants to live with moderation, one lives with moderation. If moderation is the "I am…" experidigm, then good. Still, when does moderation mean stagnation and fear of creating and fear of "I am…?" If one wants to live in the middle way, live in the middle way experidigm. As in the previous discussion in Part 3, "defining the self" can be very dangerous and constraining. If the middle way is chosen, then other ways are hidden until the experidigm evolves.

Choosing a religion can be liberating and a connecting experience, freeing the "I am…" from "you are…" torture. Focus on the liberating side of religion. Focus on connecting with the Infinite "I am…," not the administrative rules of the religion (ok, of course, the moral foundation of the Ten Commandments is not administrative rules). Let the "I am…" connect beyond the status quo of rules and create a joyful life. Those judging your beliefs never really know your beliefs, and so do not allow their stone throwing to contain the "I am…." If fear of any sort is being used by a religion to contain the "I am…," deflect that fear and connect directly with the "I am…" in the world.

Choosing the status quo is never liberating and is only stagnating. The status quo only accepts the "dumbing down" of all participants to fit into the dogma of the status quo. The status quo offers up constant "programming" to indoctrinate the group to "relax" and enjoy only what the status quo has defined as relaxing. This acceptance of the status quo and "dumbing down" of the intellect and stagnation of the "I am.." is rarely observed and understood by the status quo, so the status quo maintains and exists for very long periods. A main way to see the dumbing down caused by the status quo is to announce a new experidigm and see the mindless TTers attack.

Not all of those in the status quo are mindless. Many leaders of the status quo fully understand the intentional manipulation to create the "you are..." status quo. My book *Turd Throwers Beware* illustrates how these leaders operate. My book *Avoid Takers* further describes how the Taker cycle can enslave entire societies and their status quo. When the status quo society tells you to relax (code word to just dumb down and accept), the "I am..." should take notice and get away and create another experidigm to avoid being dumbed down.

The key to joy in this space suit is that we create our experiences and our connections, and we can do that every moment of our lives. We do not need to stagnate. Keep picking ways that do not stagnate but instead keep one connected to "I am...." Keep learning and evolving to the new experidigm.

Thanks and Gratitude

Being thankful for the joy and assistance you receive is very important to continue and grow the joy. Acknowledge keeping the joy in existence and spreading the joy to other "I am...s." Take time to know effort and notice the contributions of others. Life is not experienced alone. "Thanks" just attracts more. Thankfulness attracts love and trust connections. Gratitude is like a lubricant that keeps connections flowing and growing. Thankfulness is the glue that holds connections together. Always thank all the "I am…" connections.

As an individual, thanking frees the "I am…" and allows the "I am…" to go on to evolve the experidigm. Thanking is always positive, vanquishing the fear that holds one back. Thanking says – I accept the gift and I move forward and up. This is similar to forgiving, in that a role of forgiving is to stop thinking in the past. Forgiving, all action moves forward to the experidigm not to the past. Similarly, thank you says, "Let's keep connecting and go to the Next thank you. Thank you is for your "I am..." as much as it is for the others' "I am...."

Your Flag

As you show others your experidigms, carry each individual experidigm picture as a flag so you can show anyone and everyone and enlist them in your journey. Shine your light in front of the parade. Others can gather around you and support you. A flag serves as a center point to rally around. Others can find you and pick you out of a crowd and join you, so hold the flag and offer the flag to everyone. Do not hide your flag. When a "you are ..." attack happens, you can use your "I am..." flag in both your mind and in reality to make your "I am..." the front and center of your thought, deflecting the "you are...." Since your flag is constantly evolving and getting better, you should update it both in your mind and on the electronic page. Holding you flag high brings the support and connections one needs.

My flag is the black and white puzzle picture evolving to the color world. I see how it is now and how it will be. The puzzle pieces remind me that I need to keep making choices to get to the full color picture. Sometimes there are no good choices, so I say NEXT, like the cover of this book, and seek out new experts or different people. In the past, I have made "dream boards" as I searched for choices to add to my puzzle flag. Every day, when I start getting stuck in the status quo, I point upward with my right hand and that forces me to look up and pay attention to up. I forget the groveling in the status quo and think of my "I am...." When I do this, other people look up and say, "What are you pointing at." I explain my experidigm to them. Depending on the context, like at work, or at a meeting, others may point up with me, and we discuss how to get to the pointing. Pointing up to your flag connects you to action.

I was holding my grandson who was too young to talk, and he pointed. I pointed, and we were fully connected in spirit. Here is I that picture:

Your flag symbolizes that you are the leader of your experidigm, and everyone is looking to you for what you want to add. They want you to direct them. In *Choose Up* I talk about building skeletals of the types of choices you want in your experidigms - your skeletal can be your flag.

Your flag can be:

+ abstract

+ artistic

+ emotional

+ beautiful

+ stylistic

+ fun

+ work-related

+ social

+ giving

+ or all the above or any combination

You can have a flag for each area of your joy: for work, for hobbies, for spirit, etc. Do not just make a flag and stick with it. Add to it all the time. Here is a picture of how I view my flag and how it is like steps leading to more and more:

Some people, unfortunately, feel they should stick with the flag through thick and thin. No, the flag changes as the experidigm changes. History is a long story about building on top of the last city built on that site. We might think that what is now is all there was and is, but almost every city is built on top of another city. Use each flag and add to it or build another. They become like photographs of your life before that portion of your life happens. Start a new one or build on top of your last city.

Plant your flag at work, then plant a different one with your friends, and a different one with your family. Be joyful in building your experidigm flag. Your flag could be your dream board of all future experiences that can be imagined now, and add to when the imagination and experiences grow.

PART 7:

Education Needed

With the goal in life to be joyful by creating many experidigms with the assistance of your connections, an experidigm education would add to the Joy equation understanding and allow practice with all of the key components in the Joy equation. In most situations, current education has a broad goal of teaching basic subject matter skills, like reading, writing, arithmetic, history, some science, etc. Though useful, it is not sufficient to only teach "facts" and belief, and not address the "I am…" flow of wisdom. Experidigm education adds visualizing your future, not the end, in your mind. To create your best future, a student must be exposed to the additional key skills to achieve that best future.

Sadly, most educational systems do not teach big picture thinking and do not teach the value of "I am…" vs "you are…" actions. Education systems do not teach how to effectively live and work with others. When students graduate, most say, "What do I do now?" Of course, that is a great question. The answer to which they should have been learning and practicing potential future experidigms while in school. The NEXT question is, "How do I do it? Education would have been perfect teaching students how to connect, how to design, how to choose, how to make decisions, how to think big, and many other "how to" about their lives. Instead of learning and experimenting in school, currently, students are thrust into

133

their future life with little or no practice. The very worst of all, students are subject to extreme "you are..." and pigeonholed into a life they did not dream up and a life devoid of "I am...." With no experidigm education and skills, many get trapped in a dumbed down "you are..." life. Society and individuals can prevent this tragedy through an education program that promotes big thinking, big visualization, big connecting, and big experidigming. Specialists and educators take the world apart and then try to put it back together again, saying here are the top or key steps we need to follow to succeed in business or have a successful life. Just follow the steps, and you will arrive. That is how science portrays the world: as taking it apart and putting it back together. Most people go along with each paradigm shift science publicizes, and we try to live that way. It is like we expect to cut up the entire body, understand each part, and then put it back together again, and somehow it will be alive -- but it will not be alive; it will be completely dead. Many commercially successful and educational books have been written about tools, techniques, emotions, and thinking styles, but these dissected and spliced practices fail as a whole because they are not acting as the whole. They assume that the practices and parts come together and make an operating whole. What is needed is the big picture approach, seeing the entire picture together, experiencing it, and changing with it, and putting the stamp of individual "I am..." will on that experience. We want to stamp "I am..." on our experiences, and share these with others. Our education can show us how to make our own whole experience with our own stamp and our own flag.

Realize that the tools, the parts, or the subjects do not represent the whole. For example, using innovative tools does not guarantee that the innovation will lead to a successful whole product or business. Knowing how to use a hammer does not ensure that you can nail together a whole house. Yet, we assume that the parts world will always make our whole, and that is a delusion. Start with the whole and select the parts to fit your whole. If they do not fit, get the NEXT selection. It is always up to the individual to make and integrate the whole experience in their life. We must learn how to do that.

Do not confuse experidigming with play, or games, or goal systems. Experidigming is open ended with ever evolving futures you choose, in a timeless fashion. Playing, games, and creating goals are all closed systems, bounded by the rules created and scheduled in the artificial planned time. Your "I am..." is not bounded and has infinite choice, and infinite connections. When you bind your experidigm, you have accepted the "you are..." definition imposed upon you. Just as learning is never bounded, your experiences are never bounded and are always subject to your "I am..." choice.

Some say get off your rear end and just "jump" into the unknown, and you will learn. Learning how to survive is good, but our "I am…" is about NEXT and connecting with the NEXT and being something higher, in joy. Better to learn how to point up, connect, live the NEXT and live another NEXT. The act of jumping without a NEXT experidigm might take you out of the flow. Get into the flow.

The Role of Joy in Learning

Learning is 100% personal and directly related to the learner's desire. If learners have no desire, they may only learn by the school of hard knocks. If learners have a lifelong desire to learn in many ways, life continually opens up before them and unfolds. Learning is directly related to a person's ability to experience and connect, thus joy. The pace of learning is directly related to your connections, including school and expert mentors who share with you. The more others share with you (and reading what others wrote to share with you is considered sharing), the more you learn, and the more you can connect. Additionally, each time you connect and share, and each time you have a new experience, you are learning. Any leaning is good. Joy requires learning and creativity. Creativity comes freely from the Infinite. To truly experience joy in life, one must learn skills in three areas: 1) directed experiencing, 2) connecting and sharing, and 3) deflecting TTers and Takers. We will discuss the skills you will need in each of these areas. The online tools of the modern world will allow you to connect across physical boundaries and through different modes of thought and cultures. Understanding differences and similarities will benefit you greatly. Picture making and sharing software will assist in visioning and capturing your visual experidigm.

On Big-Picture Thinking

The Infinite, by definition, is not limited in anyway. The Infinite is pure creativity. The Infinite shares all. We just need to ask for the Infinite. Our "I am..." has access to the Infinite as we learn. Learning helps us ask for more and better. We actually get better and better at thinking big. As our learning and experience grow, we see more and we ask for more.

The problem with asking is that sometimes it is too small and almost never paints the big picture we need. We must learn to paint the big picture and think how to use all our learning and future learning to get to each big picture we create.

Traditional education teaches us to take things apart and understand them as pieces, independent from each other, and maybe understand a limited, simplistic view on how they integrate together. We are not taught integration skills at an early age. In science, we ask a "part" question (i.e. hypothesis) and then test each part to see if our question is answered. We control all the other variables to see if our simple question is answered. In math, we do each operation in a defined order. In biology, we break the animal into its parts and study each part. In English, we break sentences apart and diagram them. In any subject, we name, we define and categorize and we subcategorize.

If we do not take them apart, we summarize them with a label to simplify them. We want to be a doctor or lawyer, but that is gross over simplification. We get lost in the summary map and cannot see the details of the whole territory as one whole. We have trouble seeing how the whole fits together because we have little training on selecting and building and experience building that whole. In school we sit in chairs and think, and we lose the whole experience. Doing the experience is learning too.

We look at the details and we lose focus on the small. Our lives become small, focused on the small. Small and meaningless. Every school subject is about teaching the detail. This is Ok. However, where do we learn to look at the big picture? Where do we learn how we can impact that big picture? Better yet, when do we learn that we make our own big picture? Living by and updating the big picture should happen every day, but, normally, it is a rare day when this happens. School, church, and work – all focus on the tasks you are assigned, not the one you could create. Let me ask you – at work, when was the last time they asked you to participate in creating the work flow of which you are part? You are lucky if work ever involved you. Frankly, because you were not trained and have not learned and have no experience at big picture thinking, you are not allowed to do big picture thinking in public. That is unfortunate. Let's change that.

Acquiring big picture thinking can be learned and perfected with practice. See my book *Choosing Up*. Developing this big picture view at an early age with wisdom from elders is perfect. It is much better than just bringing parents in the classroom once a year for career day. Getting active in life as part of education begins to teach and show the flow of life. Life does not flow sitting in a chair for 18 years.

Here is how to think in the Big Picture mode…

+ as you start, create your own dream board. Cut out pictures you like from someone else's activities and paste them on your board. Make a board for work, one for school, several for your hobbies and as many as you like.

+ create a flow chart and see how things flow together. Do a flow chart for how you order something online. Do a flow chart of how you get ready to go to your first activity of the day. Learning how to prepare a flow chart is key to understanding how the whole comes together as actions flow.

+ draw a picture of how all the parts come together to make a whole, like a blow out diagram of a car engine.

+ mix and match different parts and pieces. See what you come up with and put them in a new scene from a different time of the normal day

+ scan or read 10 new books a week for new information on subject matter different than what you already know

+ Draw an experidigm for someone you have learned about. Talk with classmates about this sample and learn how to talk with them about experidigms and hear their critical views, incorporating their views into the experidigm.

If you do these simple things each week, you will understand big picture thinking. If you explain any of the output of the above activities to another, you are building your connections skills. Surely this time is better spent than watching TV, playing a video game, or just trading small talk on social media.

On Experidigming and Choice

Our free will allows for choice. If it were not for free will, life would just come and keep coming at us, like repeating and relentless ocean waves until life knocks everything over, and drags everything into the depths of the water. With free will, one has desire to do, desire to choose toward what one creates, and to not accept what keeps coming at us. We can build a boat and float over the waves, or a plane and fly, or a spaceship and soar. Free will creates choice.

Choice is not just learning how to select among the physical products in the world, though choosing and continually choosing new physical objects is a good aspect of experidigms and joy. Choice thinking and creating new thoughts and new things and processes is more important. The beauty of choice is that it is not stagnant, but adds to what exists and will exist. Choice does not exist in isolation. Although people may isolate themselves, choice is always part of infinity. The act of choosing is NEXT.

NEXT is just not taught in schools. How do we make choices? Do we just follow others in the status quo or do we blaze our own path? Choice can be closed or ignored altogether. The best way to educate about choice is to focus on how each choice is related to the experidigm. If no experidigm, then choice and free will are random, subject to the relentless ocean wave. Education can show how to make choice toward a future vision. Project and program management can be taught, but these are only tools in the toolbox to assist with focus. Much more is needed. One can teach trial and error methods for making choices for experidigms. One can teach the process of how to make experidigms and improve them.

If one is not educated and trained on how to make choices, unscrupulous people who know how to manipulate the choices of others can build choice architecture that can take advantage of another, without the target fully knowing or understanding what is happening. Just learning how to avoid manipulation from choice architecture is an important skill. Without the skill, one will be subject to very poor decisions as choice architecture takes him or her down a bad path, like buying sugar water and sugar leads to happiness (but really diabetes when in large quantities). Choices should be made in the pursuit and direction of an experidigm, not for the manufacturer pursuing you and manipulating you to buy their product. The key is to participate in choices for your experidigm and your teams' experidigms and not lose yourself in some manipulation of choice and the dilution of your desire.

Realize choice must be happening all the time as decisions are being made to flow to the experidigm. Always be testing if the choice works with the experidigm and the Joy equation. If not, make another choice - NEXT. Learning the process and the discipline to keep moving toward the "eye on the prize" experidigm is most important. This can be taught in schools with an example to actually do and practice each school year. If need be, examples may be demonstrated and tried in each subject. The prize is not the end result goal or the choice itself, but the continuous joyful flow to the experidigm with the connections. Choice is only a step up the puzzle staircase I show in the book *Choosing Up* and earlier in this Part. Getting lost means either losing sight of the experidigm or the connections, so the loss most probably was caused by a TTer trying to manipulate your choice.

Since an infinite experidigm can be created for any subject in school, each and every class can have a specific project to use choice skills. Making choices for a thought or for a thing can require different skills. Practicing and seeing all kinds of subject major choice in school is important to practice as often as possible. "Practice makes perfect." Here is how to add an experidigm to the class syllabus:

1) Have a future experidigm in each subject for each student

2) List of choices as high as 100

3) Try three choices and rate each and select three more and rate them and get rid of ones not wanted

4) Create small groups to review and have the team prepare a review for class showing how team members made their choices and how that impacted their experidigm. No need to be self-conscious about talking about an experidigm. Really need to learn how to discuss the experidigm in a non-threatening way.

5) Be who you are and learn to "sell" your experidigm to others.

All students collectively need to get better at making choices directed at their experidigms and learn to appreciate how that happens in all subjects. We can all make each other better as we flow to individual and group experidigms - all flow upward and grow together.

Can a group learn to make choices together? Of course; students can learn to make choices for a group's experidigm but thinking only with "I am…ness," not "you are…ness." A student group must learn how to create a group experidigm and the choices of the group are directed to this experidigm.

Telling and showing others your experidigm is critical to your life and all lives. Experidigms are always positive being based on "I am…." "I am…" expresses a moralistic, Ten Commandments aspiration. Why does society try to chop down and hurt aspirations (i.e. Turd Throwers)? One reason is that we have not been educated on both individual and group experidigms, how to choose them, how to respect them, and how to share them. In school, we teach criticism; we teach competition; we teach winning; we teach breaking into parts; we teach individualism…so when we show the experidigm to others, they use these currently taught skills to criticize, to compete, to win , to rip it apart, and to reward themselves for doing all these to hinder and hurt another. Instead of creating only this "win" atmosphere, education can add and point to the whole; pointing to cooperation, collaboration, and working together, not for the common goal, but for the experidigm. Long term, in-person attending schools will be about doing, practicing, meeting and connecting to learn. Whereas, on-line schools will be about presenting the basic "facts" of the subjects.

When social media first started in mid 2000s, the vast majority of stories and dialogue was supportive and positive, but as it expanded to include more and more "learned" people, the tone shifted toward judging, criticizing, competing, winning, and ripping apart. The "you are…" method is being taught and used in the public domain and is expected and rewarded. If collaborating and cooperation are not taught, the "you are…" and the Takers know no limits as to how much they can hurt and take.

Once again, if manipulative "you are…s" keep defining others and taking from them, the "I am…" and experidigm can be destroyed, so students need a crash course in deflecting TTers and building "I am…ness:"

1) State "I am…ness and deflect "you are…"

2) Build experidigm team and collaborate

3) Talk positively of "I am…ness"

These can be taught and practiced.

On Connecting and Experts

Modern education is focused on learning specific subject matter, contained in a book, and demonstrated by a teacher standing in front of the class with the expectation to offer a multiple choice test (or essay) on the subject knowledge covered. Students are rarely required to demonstrate or perform actions or physically show then know the actual experience. Students sit at their desks passively taking in the information. The test is on the book and the teacher's presentations. The test shows how much knowledge students absorb and can regurgitate on a multiple choice test. That is a passive individualistic learning approach. Normally that is the only way education is delivered until graduate school. Everything is individually based (as opposed to learning in teams), and competition versus other students for best grades is the driving force. If one gets better grades, the options for a better college or a better job are higher. Organized education promotes almost zero incentive to study, learn and work together as a group. Education has zero connection with the concept of team, collaboration or connecting with others for any reason. Formal education just does not teach working together and specifically fosters competition, not learning to work on experidigms or connecting. Sometimes, in graduate school, students work together on projects to prepare them for the real world of work. Yet, how best to work in groups is not taught. It is just expected that students get together and figure it out, or just work independently. Being taught to compete individually for years before this, then being told to suddenly work together without instruction maybe just leads to the most competitive bully taking control. Hopefully, a person's first learning experience with a group is better than bully leadership and instead focuses on allowing the different skills and perspectives of the group to be fully utilized in a potential solution. Diversity of the group can lead to a beautiful holistic experience and eye-opening solution.

Where do people become educated on how to connect and work together? Clearly, rarely in the classroom. Many receive an education through participating in team sports. In team sports, team members learn their role and to fit into that role so the team can best compete and win against another team. With teams, the role we are given is usually clearly defined and the participants learn that role, and only that role. As a team member, the role is only a part. What is learned is how to contribute and in most cases, how to win, because winning is important in a competitive "game and playing" world. Good sportsmanship is promoted as a goal, but winning is the bigger goal. Sharing knowledge and assisting others to reach goals is not necessarily part of the team. With games, wining is the only main goal although some would say the real learning is to just participate and feel the fun of participating.

Learning how to work in a group and strive for the common experidigm created by the group is a top core skill to which every person needs to be exposed, learned early in life and reinforced throughout life. Living life is a group effort. Hermits represent a very, very, very tiny portion of the population. To reach an individual or group experidigm, people must learn to share their different knowledge and skills in the direction of their visualized future. This can be taught and reinforced with practice. In *Choosing Up* a student can see sample action strips for a group to work on together in creating and designing a future experience. The group may use their individual expertise to discuss the many action strips associated with the experience. To practice, a group can select a future experidigm to create and then focus their discussion on making and improving that future. Later in this Part, a chart shows a summary of what types of activities (or action strips) can be focused upon by school year of students.

If structured education would teach and show how to work together on experidigms, students will become good at it and be able to practice teamwork in a non-competitive, connected way. Can you picture that students get good at collaborative work for their own benefit and for the benefit of the group? Constructive dialogue would be a foundation of how we communicate, not the "you are…" manipulation dominating the modern world.

What would the educated look like if education added how to connect and work together? Each educated person would know how to read and write sentences and know basic math. Yes, the public school system has that today. If we are taught how to connect, we would be able to share each individual experidigm and other people would actually care and might participate. Best of all, student participation would be very meaningful based on their team education and adding their unique knowledge, expertise and experience. They would be able to share a meaningful dialogue, and not spout "you are…" and block all progress. They would be able to ask questions and contribute to the understanding and needs that an Oudit target comparison might suggest. They would want to meet with the team at intervals to review and make sure progress is happening and that joy was being experienced. They would not be competing to take the joy away for themselves or to take the joy and horde it.

Science is taught in a way to take things apart and understand how the pieces work together. Now, from being connected with various experts, and knowing how to work together, an experidigm can take a holistic future view and respect the perspectives and differences of all the connections. The holistic view is driving the discussion. The connections are able to evolve their discussion as the change in the context and environment can change the experidigm. Both the experidigm and the connections are an evolving and living process. Aliveness and flow are part of the connections and drive the connections, unlike competition and the desire to win driving the connections. We can build living connections in the schools as students learn, write, speak, play and work.

Competition is good with playing where the rules structure the environment and flow. Connecting is core to learning and living. Connecting is an action, and it is focused on talking, visualizing, creating, and doing in the context of the larger experidigm. Connected participants are part of the whole and still independent for their own experidigms. Being connected in a nurturing and caring way with other experidigms is critical for collaborative and peaceful human history.

Cooperation can build a common experidigm. Competition, if allowed to break the world into parts and pit them against each other, can be devoid of life. Life flows with wholeness. Competition can flow with wholeness as well, and this can lead to joyful experidigms for all, beyond mere parts and winning. We can compete and respect wholeness and connections. When competition is completed and is followed by "you are…" actions, the completion was not performed in the spirit of connection. Any "you are…" spirit is meant to hurt or subjugate an "I am…."

Teaching the ability to connect and share and build an experidigm allows an individual and a community to grow overcoming the bully tendency to control and take.

On Deflecting TTers and Avoiding Takers

The book *Soaring to Awesome – Turd Throwers Beware* describes how intentionally hurtful people (TTers) try to keep people in the status quo. TTers use proven approaches to prevent differences and changes from manifesting. The book also teaches how to overcome TTers in a loving and caring way to reach an individual or group experidigm. Learning how to overcome TTing behavior is critical to practicing experidigming while receiving an education. For many people, going to school and eating/sleeping with their family is the overwhelming majority of life from 5 to 18 years old. At school, many different cultures, social groups, and perspectives come together, some vying for "you are..." supremacy and control. This attempt at control will impact every student at some time during education, and, in most cases, many times, even bordering on daily bullying. Part of education should be how to deflect TTers with love and care in the deflecting heart. Here is the summary deflecting shield from *Soaring to Awesome* that shows the six types of Turd Throwers:

The ability to deflect TTers directly impacts the ability to receive joy in life. This is core to living an "I am..." life. Deflecting TTers is as important as connecting to the Joy equation. In education, teaching deflecting and connection can happen while individuals work and learn in teams together. Both good and bad methods can be shown and acted out.

In addition to teaching deflection, education can also show how to avoid intentional manipulation and enslavement caused by the Taker Cycle (see book entitled *Avoid Takers*). As discussed in *Avoid Takers*, manipulation can occur when an "I am..." attempts to deliver a potential solution for a Takers' problem, but the Taker enslaves the "I am..." continually asking for more. Normal "I am...ers" can be trapped in a cycle of trying to solve the Taker problem. This cycle picture below summarizes how the Taker traps the "I am..." and how the "I am..." must say "No!" and be firm at saying and keeping "No!"

Taker Cycle

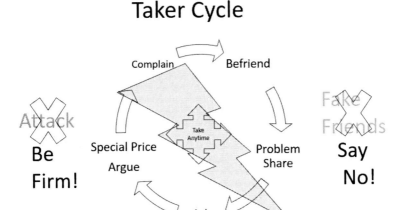

On Being in Flow

Life flows. If flow happens, life happens, and if flow continues, life continues. Our focused attention and action can enhance flow and create more flow. We can participate in designing how our future flows. We can learn how to have input into our life flow. Stagnation causes disease and death, and obvious cessation of flow. Individuals are not fully in control of the flow around them, nor are individuals in control of the exact flow of their life, but individuals can put energy into directing choices, and these choices can positively impact the flow in life. Choices can take one closer to the best experidigm vision or away from it. Making choices is the course corrector in life. Experience can be the input to redirect the flow in life, so the flow goes toward the current experidigm. Choice impacts connections, experiences, and deflecting TTers, all the components of the Joy equation.

In a flowing world, choices keep adding up to more joy, to more complexities, to more experiences. The emphasis of flow is on what we experience, not necessarily on how one performs in that experience. Playing the piano technically perfect is probably not joy, but experiencing and living in the melody might be joy. Being in the experience moment of doing is joy. Getting a grade on how we perform that experience is something else. Life is not a performance to be judged, but to be lived as a flow we intentionally have a part in designing. As such, we are part of the flow. Teaching flow as part of human nature is positive.

Flows connect and interact and blend together. Flow togetherness occurs on both the physical and the energetic level. Some prediction of what might happen when flows combine may be based on past experience, but experience is a non-stop blending of infinite possibility, so exact prediction is not possible. Joy is possible. Infinite flow means our experience is always open for new experidigms and refreshing new joy. If more flow experiences are sought out, new and unique flows can result. This will always be so, or at least until all flows, all infinite ends. Infinite multiplied by infinite is still infinite.

Interestingly, flow brings new parts into existence. While life flows, new parts and new possible choices are always being brought into existence. When flows collide, they bring new choices. One can intentionally have one's experidigm flow connect and collide with other experidigm flows as shown in this wave connecting picture.

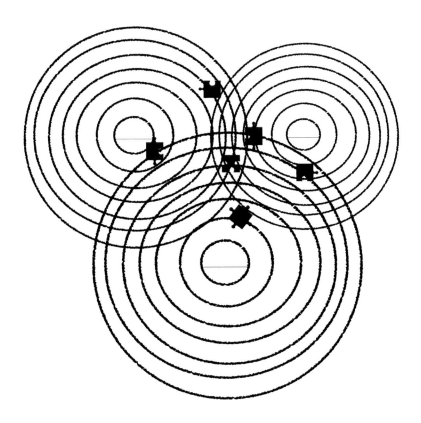

The connection and collision ignites learning. This sounds hard, but this is as easy as looking at your future experidigm and comparing it to someone else's experidigm. Or, this is just adding "experts" with a different point of view to your team, and having them recreate your experidigm, and you pick the best new parts. In this case, flow is an intentional act made in the direction to alter your experidigm. How complex this process is made is solely up to the person redesigning their experidigm. Just desire to create and build a new experience and get in the flow of doing and connecting.

You can design the flow and see how that works. The reality is you will probably need to adjust the flow. Flows are never perfect. Distractions and setbacks will happen, so keep flowing. Grades are not handed out for a life well lived, so just live well.

The educational point is that individuals enter a flow in a directed way and learn how to add to, subtract from, and improve on as they shift the direction toward an experidigm. Learning NEXT is happening all the time. NEXT is always in front of us and we can learn how to engage NEXT that best suits us. The perfect right is only fleeting, as the NEXT is waiting a split second later to offer up the flow to joy.

Asking the question, "What are the sequential steps necessary to be in flow?" is really a silly question. This is similar to taking live things apart and putting them back together again and thinking they will be alive. Either become part of the steps or part of the flow, only flow leads to living. Steps are too limiting and close ended. Just point to your experidigm and know NEXT exists and share connections. Connections can be all these types of words all at once: cooperation, teamwork, sharing, relating, caring and loving. All these aspects exist in the flow of connection.

Flowing toward an experidigm can be taught and practiced.

On Comparing vs Targets

In Part 5 we saw how each experidigm can be measured versus a target and any deviations can be noted and reviewed to see how to make the experidigm better. One of the most important activities in life is to compare how we are doing now with the future visual experidigm. Based on that comparison, what adjustments and connections should be made. Sharing this comparison with others to see if our proposed adjustments are valid or are they adjustments based on delusional and constrained thinking. Can one reach higher and further? Should we add more flow experidigms different from the one currently being used? In the business world, this is called an audit, where independent 3rd parties come into the business and see if the business is performing to its stated targets and using generally accepted business practices. Audits should not be reserved only for business. Individuals should have their own comparison and target tracking process I call Oudit target comparison. Oudit is the process by which individuals evaluate where they are now with their target experidigm, and make the needed adjustments to get to the target or readjust the target.

Schools can teach the Oudit process every year in school. Schools can teach the importance of having an experidigm, and where you are related to it, and how to adjust based on the comparison. Students can practice using the Oudit process when they work on any school projects. The most important reason to Oudit is to check your experidigm in light of a changing world and ask: "should I improve my experidigm and what do I need to add, do, share, or create to my experidigm?

Checking how the experidigm flow is going with the Oudit process is not a goal setting process with milestone and targets. Goals and milestones are for project management of coordinating a team to create a new product or business. A life, an "I am...," and an experidigm is not a project to achieve, to have a completion date and then stop and relax. Use Oudit in a constant process to keep your experidigm fresh and evolving, and joy can be fresh and evolving in all aspects of life. Just as it is hard to fully understand confusing words in prayer and treatment and then have a connected "I am..." understand, it is hard for the connected "I am..." to participate in goals and milestones. The "I am..." is connected for as long as the "I am..." visualization is understood, and project timelines and milestones have no meaning to the "I am...." Time is meaningless to "I am...."

Schools can teach Oudit comparison just as schools teach creating and selecting experidigms.

On Asking Questions

The Oudit process can be simple or very detailed and comprehensive. The process starts with picking an area of the experidigm life to compare with a "best practice of doing." "I want to do …, and this is similar to…., so I will use this as my target to compare with each time period (i.e. week)." For example, I want better health and I will compare my physical health to the *Men's Health* or *Women's Health* magazine average person and his or her associated exercise habits. The average person does certain exercises a day, and I will compare myself to that. Data can be collected by hand in diaries or by using sensed data into cell phones or both.

Some schools have arrived at a point where the majority of students just do not ask questions or risk asking questions. When school grades are based on getting the right multiple choice answer, the quest for the right answer is the goal, not asking and learning. There is only black or white, right or wrong, with no grey area and no need for questions. Study the list of material, memorize it and replay it on the test. Conformity is at a premium, and questioning takes a back seat. Getting great grades, almost a 4.0, is the goal so the student can get into a prestigious college, and then after college get a prestigious job. There is not really the need for questions, given the strict regimen and only one right answer. Just memorize that one answer. If questions are asked, that might shine a negative light and reflect badly on getting the prestigious placements. The art of asking questions is not learned or practiced in schools. In some cases, asking questions makes one look stupid, so even if questions are needed, asking them is avoided to look "smart."

The main way to improve joy is to ask questions about experidigms and to ask those connections who can assist with the questions. Understanding, improvement and action occur because questions are asked. Learning how to ask questions is a core life skill to capture and evolve joy. Joy equation experience and connections can be improved by asking questions. Asking also tells the asker if the connection is an "I am…" sharer who works toward understanding the asker or a Taker who switches most questions toward the Taker need, not the asker need.

Asking questions to connections is not personal. Feeling any emotional response to the answer should be avoided - feeling of being stupid is the asker being delusional. The reality is that if the answer does not move forward the experidigm or the connections, then move to the next question that will move forward to the experidigm. To recruit connections, one must ask them questions. If they appear helpful, then ask them to contribute more. Here are some simple questions that can be asked over and over again:

+ How do I... do, see, act...?

+ What do you...think, know, experience...?

+ Can you...get, share, do, help...?

+ What improvements...?

+ Best way...?

Asking questions is always safe. Questions invite others into your flow of joy.

The Experidigm Methodology

At a minimum, the Experidigm Methodology consists of ten core skills to be taught and practiced. In the list below the title of the skill is listed first, followed in parentheses () by a summary word for the skill, and lastly followed by the actual skill to be demonstrated by doing.

1. The Principles of Pointing Up (Focus) – "I am..."

2. The Wholeness of the Picture (Seeing) – Sketch/Photo

3. The Science of Selecting (Choice) – Skeletal/Maps

4. The Leadership to Connect Experts (Team) – Program

5, The Act of Integrating (Combine) – Marshalling/logistics

6. The Joy of Flowing (Doing) – Joy Equation

7. The Oudit Comparison (Target) – Progress

8. The Platform Step Evolution (Experidigm) - Stairs Up

9. The Deflection of Delusions (TTers) – Shield

10. No excuses or Stagnation (NEXT) – Overcome

In previous discussions I have shown how ripples and waves from "I am…" people come together to share puzzle pieces and other information.

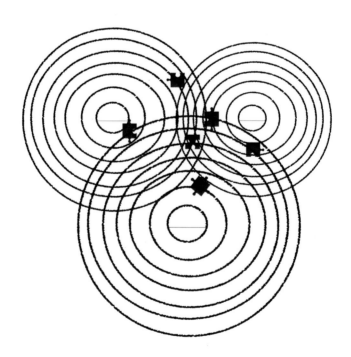

The notion these pictures share is that "I am…" people share their knowledge to assist each other to improve their experidigms. The simple notion was to show others can expand your selections (i.e. component #3 above) and assist making a better experidigm. Using the same thought process, the picture below shows the waves as the 10 components of The Experidigm Method.

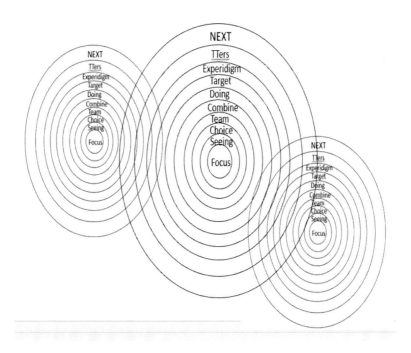

Now, when the waves are shared among those educated in The Experidigm Method, any and all of the components can be shared among "I am…ers."

Another way to look at this simple waves picture is to view it as a bullseye, with the center being the focus of the "I am…" experidigm. The core of life is to focus on the "I am…" and receive the Joy equation. As discussed earlier, the Oudit comparison process helps to ensure the focus is on the bullseye of the target.

Education by School Age

Using the ten key skills above, the chart below shows how the ten skills should evolve as one progresses through a traditional education system. At the conclusion of each school year the student should be able to show their participation in visualizing, connecting, and creating and experidigm while deflecting TTers.

	Grade School	High School	College
Focus	Unique "I am"	I am+I am = We am	We am = big group
Seeing	Drawing Future	Visual Stories	Interactive Visuals
Choice	Skeletal to whole	Maps	Multivariate
Team	Playing & friends	Group projects	Multi discipline
Combine	Assemble to whole	Design and Use	Sustainability
Doing	Play	Play Context	Context prototype
Target	List and check	Best Comparison	Real time IoT
Experidigm	Build game	Major project	Prototype offered
Deflect	Say I am, no You	TTer shield practice	Defect & avoid
NEXT	Improve game	Improve project	Improve prototype

Raising Kids

Luckily, no book on how to raise a child comes along with the child's delivery at the time of birth. Sounds funny, but everything we buy comes with an how to manual. The reason products and things come with a manual is the thing we buy does not have an "I am..." will. A child has an "I am..." will and can experidigm. As parents and as society, our role to teach children is to allow them the free open spaces to learn how to connect and experidigm for a life time. Understanding how to do big-picture thinking, how to make many choices for joy, and how to share to build experidigms are the keys to life. Children must be exposed to these as early as possible.

Kids have a natural "I am…" tendency that wants to joyfully explore and experience. Children want to share these experiences with a smile on their face. Even before children talk, they are exploring and sharing toys. How to keep this joy going for children in the modern world is a challenge. A common notion is that children must be protected, and to do this some build a proverbial wall around the child and the child does learn; thereby teaching children fear and mistrust. Learning environments must abolish these walls. If we keep inadvertently teaching fear, the "I am…" is trapped in a "You are…" corner. Education must allow for exploring experidigms and connections free from fear. The role of a parent is to make sure these joy keys of life do not get buried under the "you are…' of life. The "I am…" needs to flourish and expand into open spaces. Perhaps families must build community play areas and use them to explore individual and group experidigms.

Future Open Spaces

In the not-too-distant past, people were able to get out, get away and explore the outdoors because there was free open space in which to expand. In these open spaces people could feel free, limitless and connected to something bigger than themselves. One could expand into the openness and grow. One could make mistakes and learn in this openness, without being negatively judged and having their future progress blocked by mistakes. While you can still pay to get into a government park where there is beauty and open spaces, there are also hordes of tourists restricting the individuals' freedom. Where are the modern open spaces into which one may expand freely?

New open spaces (well, not really new but more useful with the loss of physical open spaces) are found in your mind and shared online and connected online. Imagination and vision create open spaces. This was always so, but now you can share those creative open spaces easily online, across geographical and physical barriers. You can create and design all aspects of your experience and select all your best choices. You can collaborate with experts and your team. You have infinite free space. You change and you change your free space.

You might say your imagination is not real. But your imagination is what connects and leads to your experidigms and becomes real. Some call this the law of attraction, but it is much bigger than that. It is the Infinite "I am...."

You can build physical areas and rooms to test how your imagination plays out in a real context. This is full immersion contextual experience. Change the context and see how it changes the experience.

PART 8:

Living Experidigm Life

Joy is captured as one flows to the experidigm and participates to make the experidigm happen. Sometimes the joy is felt immediately when the flow starts (i.e. runners' high) or when the experidigm has been achieved (i.e. graduating from college). Even those activities which push one very hard to the brink of endurance can be looked back upon with extreme joy. Like walking or running or bike riding up a long arduous hill and stopping to catch breath, pushing oneself, being the "little engine that could." Hating every step of the way to the top, but when one gets to the top and looks around, one feels the absolute joy of getting there, arriving. And, if you shared it with your connections in person or online, being on the top feels that much better as you share and spread the experidigm.

Pursuing the experidigm is like gardening. Preparing the land and planting is hard work, but with patience, and continued daily work on weeding and watering, the food comes up, and like standing at the top, the joy of eating is experienced.

I am not saying that hard work and effort are required. Hard work and effort is a process, and as one does the process, one needs to remain creative and open to the connections to improve both the process and the experidigm. NEXT time in the garden, one plants even more variety of plants as other experts instruct the gardener. Or one climbs to a taller top NEXT time with more ease based on connected assistance.

Beauty

The most beautiful thing a space suit can do is smile and share. The most beautiful thing an "I am..." can do is love and share. Both smiling and loving are joyful connections of the "I am...."

Living in no judgment is a beautiful connection. No judgment permits infinite creativity and sharing in your "I am..." connections. These connections have tangible access to NEXT. After you attain a NEXT, you use you discernment to use it in the way your "I am..." points to your individual Experidigm.

The most beautiful action is a connected experience flowing to another connected experience. Flowing in the "I am..." connection is like receiving high fives all day long.

Beauty is pretty simple. Smile and share.

Morality

Living with morality is as simple as living with beauty. Just love. Love yourself, love others like yourself, and love the infinite connection. For those who need a list to check off to test if they are moral, use the Ten Commandments from the Old Testament of the Bible or some other religious list of a few basic moral laws. The reality is that if one loves others, laws like the Ten Commandments are just lived as part of love. The foundation of living an 'I am...' life is this basic morality of love and simple love based rules like the Ten Commandments. A "you are...' life has no basic foundation, no morality, and no love, just taking and manipulation others to believe they are better because they give to you.

Without simple morality, society breaks down into "you are.." and the desire of the "you are…" to legislate laws and make very grey area definitions that allow taking, and takers can define good taking ways (i.e. maybe some form of value trading that largely flows to the Takers' because they are smarter – a version of "buyer beware") as opposed to bad taking. The thing about laws is that they are sort of the minimum requirement before all hell breaks loose, like being the guardrails on a cliff side road. As long as you can stay within the guardrails, all actions are ok. Laws do not create law-abiding citizens – traffic driving laws do not create good drivers. If true freedom is only protected by laws, and not morals, then law-based freedom will devour true freedom with amoral laws to protect the status quo "you are…." Status quo laws can devour freedom and enable "you are…" dominance. The only way true freedom exists is through a simple, moralistic "I am…" love and respect connected to the Infinite.

The Joy equation is based on a foundation of morality flowing from individual responsibility. This responsibility creates love in the spirit of connecting to, collaborating for and experiencing the experidigm future. While we live in these space suits, we are responsible for creating and evolving to "I am…" futures in collaboration with other "I am…ers." This is not so hard. What is hard and amoral is deciding to be a disconnected "you are…" Taker.

Checklist

Living in flow is a bit like an Easter egg or scavenger hunt. You know you are hunting, but really know nothing else, like where items for which you are searching might be or what color they are. Even with the lack of specifics, it is best to take the leap and start the hunt. You will learn and adjust as you go. Similarly, the process of experidigming is like a hunt. You create your first hunt for the first experidigm; you go and you design and find it. You find one, and you want more. That is how life is when it flows. Flow feeds on flow and more flow happens. But, the hunt must be started.

Sometimes the hunt is stopped because of being lost or something breaks (i.e. an egg gets stepped on). Just keep on moving and searching. Sometimes we set the full bag of eggs down, turn away to a distraction, and somebody takes all the eggs from the bag. That happens, but there is more searching to do. So search some more. Some others say "you are stupid," and expect all stupid people to stop. No reason to listen to these "you are…" people. Keep going. Doing several searches at the same time increases joy.

Searching becomes easier and easier.

This little search example seems so trivial, but flow is like this. Just keep with it. Here is a summary page checklist which helps to highlight what to focus on…this is the "Experidigm Checklist':

Accomplish in Order	Check
Declare "I am…" using Free Will	
Visualize two example experidigms	
at play	
at work	
Pick helpful and expert teams	
at play	
at work	
Select choices for each experidigm	
Compare choice results with target	
Evolve to NEXT	

Living Experidigms

Experidigms can come in all shapes and sizes. In *Choosing Up* I show in Part 9 how to design experidigms for specific experiences. In addition, below I summarize some action flow areas that can be designed as experidigms. With each flow area joy can be captured:

+ +sports and exercising: Get into the action and be part of the action and flow. Picture yourself performing at a high level or a fun level. Learn how to play and how to challenge current performance. Reach to newer, higher, and "funnier" levels of performance.

+ +culture-art-music-writing-acting: Be part of the heartbeat of the emotions while playing and participating with others in the act or in the audience.

+ +work: Creating experiences and servicing the customer is the core to breaking the routine of work. Work is the flow of connection with the customer, or the flow of tasks, or the flow with people. If one gets in the flow, all the actions of the flow can be as designed in the experidigm.

+ +enjoying friends and family: Building things and going places and being together while doing have limitless experidigms.

+ +playing: Playing can be the easiest way to have an experidigm experience because we create the rules for the game, and we can successfully live within these rules. We can control how we live within the rules.

+ +education, reading, and learning: Visualizing the design of the future and how that future will be means access to knowledge, whether from education, from reading about newness, or from connecting The ability to do is commensurate with one's ability, and one can change and improve one's ability through education and learning.

+ +thought and intentions and prayer: The human mind can visualize any experience and share that experience with other minds. In so doing, a shared experidigm comes into existence.

Combining the few areas listed above can lead to an infinite number of actions and experidigms.

Journey Map

In todays' business world, companies are talking about what the "journey map" that a customer must follow to be able to buy a product. Let's make this journey map simple and easy for the customer. To build a journey map, what are the touchpoints that the company must have with the customer? In the most simplistic viewpoint, the touchpoints are: 1) build awareness and understanding before the purchase, 2) enable the purchase, 3) deliver the purchase, 4) follow up with questions and service, and 5) repeat with more purchases. This seems simple enough. The company can create an online program to make contact with the customer at each step of the journey with automatic emails and other social media to direct the customer and ensure that customers are still on their journey.

Can a journey map be used to plot out the path of life with all the evolving experidigms? Can the touchpoints be described with our connected team? Perhaps. The journey to an evolving experidigm is easy as we know. Picture it; share it; do it; improve it, and do it again and repeat, as often as one likes. Although, the reality is that an experidigm is not a journey, it is an experience, many experiences. We are always in the experience. We are not really on a journey. We are on a path, because we are moving, but that does not mean we have a destination in mind and we are then done. With experidigming, we are never done; we are always experiencing joy—hopefully. NEXT.

Somewhat reluctant to use the concept of journey with an experidigm. Journey sounds positive, but conveys a notion of always on our way, not really arriving, always pushing off joy until sometime in the future, but never actually getting anything. Why should a journey be good, when I can experience joy right now, and keep experiencing joy? A journey brings up images of moving physically from here to there, but not really feeling anything on the journey. A journey begins with the first step, the fist motion- so what - who cares about the obvious? Motion is not being part of the flow, and a journey is just motion. A journey does not mean action either. Action and flow are part of the experience of doing. A journey is not necessarily part of experience. Sure, people go on a journey to have experiences; people do not go on an experience to have a journey. Experience is part of the Joy equation; a journey is not. A journey is just the passage of time to go from here to there, like flying from LA to NYC in a plane. On that journey, there might be some transactions that make the journey possible, but these are not experiences for the Joy equation. Journey is only the passage of time. Those who want to put in time like a journey can stagnate and become addicted to the journey at the same time. Stagnation and addiction are bad and must be avoided. Create an experidigm to overcome the stagnant impact of a journey.

Timing of Infinite

There is no time bounding your "I am...." When the "I am..." is creating, in that instant, it is timeless and accesses all time as the "I am..." participates in the infinite. Time is not physical although we have created analogies of time with our clocks measuring the cycles we observe in nature around us. Our physical description of time helps us experience in our physical space suits, but nonetheless our definition is like our space suits—they both will die. It is good to create things like time to enable our experiences. This type of creation does not necessarily create time, it only serves our experience if we want. Time is not the important thing--our experience is more important.

Love without Judgment

Most people would readily agree that love and nonjudgment would allow us all to live in a peaceful world and set a great foundation for us to connect with our "I am...s." All people will say they have love in them. This is so because everyone does have an "I am...." We are all able to love and be non-judgmental, not just for an instant, but for every moment of our lives. So, what happens?

You would be right to say that "you are..." type people play with love words and actions to enslave others. We must understand this and not let that into our "I am...." But even without "you are..." people, we would still be challenged if our focus was on words and not experiences. Love is an experience and a connection, not words. Words and language have a built in duality: love and hate. Words have adjectives in which to convey varying levels of judgment. If one really only uses words to express love, one will be missing the mark. Love is only felt and sensed in the action and experience, not the words. Words will quickly slip into judgment, and be careful that the NEXT words out of your mouth to your lover are 'You are....' It is far better to say "let us experience...."

Words and intent are not the real thing. Words try to point to the thing, but they are not the thing. Words can never contain the wholeness of love, but your experience and connections can. You can experience love in your sharing, doing, eating, praying, kissing, etc.

Giving is not the same as sharing and is not necessarily loving. If the giving is removed from the direct contact of the sharing experience, the giving then can be shallow and only a proxy for love, like I checked love off the list, and I am now ok.

Loving yourself is the act of experidigming and connecting to "I am...."

Overcome Human Bias

Humans are not perfect. Our space suit machine works well enough most of the time to experience life. Our mind is good, but has individual types of bias that simplify and can trap our mind into certain ways of thinking without us really knowing we are trapped. For instance, we tend to delude ourselves that we are right, in the face of evidence that we are wrong--but then again, maybe we were right? Bias is a mind simplifying exercise. Some of these biases can push us toward making mistakes or behaving poorly or make us susceptible to being manipulated as a "you are...." It is important to know how to overcome biases. Being connected with different opinions and testing, doing and experiencing in the direction of an evolving experidigm will overcome bias. Action and connection expose bias in both mental and physical realities we observe, and the bias difference we note can be addressed and changed in relation to our experidigm. The "I am..." can create reality. While there may be a disparity between your future experidigm and the now reality, and as we move toward the new future, the Oudit comparison will note bias and other changes that may be required. The "I am..." will guide you to the best situation even though your mind is biased and your body not perfect. "I am..." connects and collaborates to understand many perspectives at once, and makes appropriate choices to coordinate with the experidigm.

Bias is a human weakness. A larger bias for each individual is the bias everyone has in accepting the status quo and promoting behaviors to protect the status quo, even at the risk of harming others who challenge the status quo.

Another very dangerous bias is the naïveté to believe others: when in fact, they may be actively manipulating most participants and taking from them. In the modern world of online computing, "choice architecture" herds people into making certain decisions that they want people to make, like buying a specific product. This is improved in real-time by doing comparison testing (i.e. A-B testing) and selecting the best alternative to focus the user in the right direction. Picture a cow being pushed down a specific corral, and the cow yells MOOOOO! (which means I do not want to go this way) but the path is already chosen by the rancher and the cow is lead to the slaughter (i.e. purchase.).

Lastly, a bias towards joy is perfection. Have a bias for experidigming and connecting (and, of course, loving).

Modern Day Slavery

When the "you are…" mentality dominates society and ensures the status quo operates (i.e. passing protectionism laws) as a "you are…," bully institutionalized slavery takes over. A "you are…" mindset has no limits, and enslaving entire societies is within that no limit zone. This slavery is "allowed" by the citizen slaves when they are given some level of freedom, satisfaction they can call their own, like watching sports and partying on the weekends. Modern day slavery occurs when a person's definition of them self is owned by another organization, whether it is by the government, a bank note, a school loan, a retail company credit card, a company employee, a medical bill, or a media pronouncement. Sobering revelation occurs when freedom has been redefined and accepted as living in and by the definition of the enslaver who has a claim to the definition of the person. Society can even administer a personality test to determine what type of definition you belong to now and build a plan to further enslave you. Social media big data can join the enslavement and sells to enslavers how to further enslave and direct one's choices. Misinformation points to the one enslaved as the enslaver and the enslaver as the victim. The white man is the victim of the "savage" native Indian as the victim fights back to truly enslave and be the victor of the savage Indian. And to the victor belongs the spoils – sounds like a clear Taker cycle strategy.

Slavery has normally been viewed as it relates to physical ownership of a human being and that human being is used to perform work with all the output going to the enslaver. "Legal" contracts supported by society were used to **define** the slave as physical property. Most of the world now recognizes that "you are my slave and property" is morally wrong. Sad to say that new forms of "you are… and your mind and output are my property as slave" now exist. These new forms of enslavement can be based on "legal" contracts (i.e. financial slavery), or based on mental manipulation (i.e. electronic media). In each of these cases, the "I am…" person is redefined by the "you are…" and gets enslaved by the Taker cycle, with little hope of actually emerging as a fully free "I am…er."

Physical slavery is clear, easily understood and identified. One can see when another is physically constrained and imprisoned, and has little option but to do what the "owner" says. The modern world is more sophisticated and creates definitional contracts that require the once free contract signers to spend large portions of their life spending their time and actions abiding by the terms of the contract. Borrowing money for a house, for school, for things to live with, or a car can cause one to be in financial slavery for one's entire life, paying the majority of what they make, when they make it. At the end of 2015, the average person in the USA had a household debt (i.e. credit card, auto and school) of $91,000 and mortgage debt of $168,000 (source Huffington Post 5-23-2107), with a total debt of almost $260,000. Over the last 10 years the median household income (source USA census) was around $55,000 and the average household expense (source USA Bureau of Labor Statistics) was $50,000 (including mortgage payment), so each average family has $5,000 per year to pay off the $91,000 debt. Assuming no salary increase and no interest rate on debt, it would take 91,000/5,000 = 18.2 years to pay off the household debt if nothing changes (and realize it will also take 30 years of income to pay off the mortgage debt). The average person lives for about 20 years to pay off debt, and if something goes wrong, like health issues or major loss with no insurance or the loss of a job, the number of years can extend dramatically. If something continues to go wrong, the debt cannot be paid and thus the family files for bankruptcy protection at a rate over one million bankruptcies per year. Clearly, this modern slavery is not trivial.

A critic would surely say borrowers made choices to enslave themselves; they bought the house, they bought the education, they bought the car; they bought that life – they made the choices. On the surface that is correct. They made the choices – based on the information one has at the time of the choice with only a belief and hope for the future. No one knows how the future will turn out. Sometimes life treats us well, sometimes not. As we know with experidigms, we move to them directionally and we choose, adjust, and evolve to experidigms as conditions warrant, yet a legal contract leaves little room for adjustment. The legal contract is the condition.

The real question related to the modern world: is it really the individual free choice or the will and laws of the "you are…" society. Are society, and the "you are…" dominant definitions of that society being made in such a way as to funnel the majority of people the way of the status quo? Picture the cow "moooooooing" as it is corralled into the slaughterhouse watching TV. Better yet, picture the sales team funneling the customer to the status quo product, or the social media big data team armed with precise personal data to manipulate a consumer down a purchase path, showered by emails, texts, tweets, etc. Sure the consumers make a choice because they need a place to live, they need a ride to get to work, they need to eat, they need health attention, and they need an education. Even if one has a choice, who in the "you are…" world is looking out for and collaborating with the individual to ensure they are being treated morally and not just the subject of constant buyer beware? The moral of this story is do not get defined by the "you are…" financial and commercial slavery of the modern world. When a person accepts the "you are…" will of another and uses that to substitute for their own "I am…," the taker begins the Taker cycle and takers have no limits to how much they can take.

How is the "I am…" doing to avoid the 'you are…" modern slavery of debt? Not so well. One of the American dreams of the modern world was "to get a good college education and this lands a good paying job." As more and more people have gone to college, and with colleges raising tuition, the debt for students has risen dramatically in ten short years and now is a significant portion of household debt. That is staggering, considering student debt was just a blip on the scene twenty years ago. Now add to this debt the picture of high levels of unemployment for college grads. Not a pretty picture. The students bought the "you are..." delusion of taking student debt to get a better job. Did they really have a choice, as college tuitions rose and businesses automated and eliminated jobs? Instead, maybe an "I am..." experience could have worked with connections to build a better life, connected and living responsibly with each other, connected in a community, and not alone with debt. Financial slavery and physical slavery define the victim in the same way – reduced freedom and joy.

How is the "I am..." doing to avoid the 'you are...' modern slavery of electronic manipulation of ones' choice and ones' "you are...persona"? Not so well. Think selling identity information and "identity theft," and that few people are fully aware that they are being sold. Behind the computer screen, all the online information from a person is used to create an artificial defined identity or persona, and based on the new "you are..." persona, the "you are..." will target you with communication after communication to increase the chances that the "slave" consumer picks the choice as the master defined. The "you are..." constantly and instantly correct their data on each person as the person does anything online. The "you are..." adjust and improve how they try to manipulate the choices of each persona. The modern terminology for this process is called "choice architecture" -- where electronic flow systems move the "slave" consumer through a specific flow of choices -- to the choice marketers want the slave to make:

+ for businesses – to buy my product or service

+ for government – to pay all your taxes when owed

+ for media – to create stories and manipulate eyes and ears for advertising dollars

This is the power of manipulation caused by the "you are..." on a mass manipulation scale. A mass 'you are..." delusion can maintain the status quo of society.

Say it is not so. Ok, it is not exactly like "big brother" in the novel by George Orwell called *1984*. No *1984* "big brother" really needs to watch you because big brother can define you exactly as "you are.." and market that "you are..." to you and make you feel "you are...," as you make the choices being "architected" to you. You feel "free," but you were defined and manipulated. I wonder? Is working all week to afford watching sports (i.e. football) on TV for the weekend while drinking poisonous sugar water and alcohol, eating prefabricated food like snacks, then taking pharmaceuticals at night to counteract the diabetes, heart disease and cancer considered freedom? Is this the picture created by a "you are..." who took all the money from people to support this TV dream, or the picture of an "I am..." experidigm connected to other "I am..." and the Infinite "I am...?" No 'I am...ers" ever picture an experidigm intentionally hurting themselves or others. No matter. An "I am..." can choose the Joy equation at any time, even if under slavery and make the new experience to a joyful life.

Understanding how one is being manipulated is very important. Modern day slavery is as real as the discussion above. Making manipulation worse is the growing trend by major news media outlets to fragment and focus their attention on smaller and smaller target markets so that the targeted media may not be presenting the unbiased news, but instead presenting 1) targeted infomercials or 2) propaganda "you are..." scripted opinions to which the target audience is receptive. Reporting what has happened is now secondary to offering infomercials and scripted "you are..." opinions. Each news media outlet has an affiliation with their target group, whether the group is political (i.e. Republican, Democratic, etc.), or based on sexual orientation, based on religion, or based on nationality. Each target group has its status quo and definitions that make the group who they are. Of course, each status quo group tells stories about how the other different groups are "you are..." unacceptable. Manipulation is becoming so widespread in culture with ads, infomercial media, slavery, religions of fear and strong status quos, the free will and "I am…" is challenged continually and needs the Turd Thrower deflection shield.

Explore and find the "I am…" soul with which everyone is borne.

Trapped

One can get trapped in the delusion that hard work, sweat equity, and believing in the "American Dream" handshake of a promised future job will pay off with one receiving ownership, partnership, executive status or some other high privilege. The sales pitch for the trap goes something like this: "you are one of many 'smart people' for the 'partner position' and if you work hard and long hours, one day you break through and become 'a partner owner.'" Sure, some very few break through to partner, but this trap delusion just contributes to the wealth of the current owners, who get dedicated low cost labor working hard, and keep cycling the newly educated into the trap as elders "who failed to make partner" leave.

Here is how the "false aspirational" game is played in those industries that offer many people hard work and the delusion to enter the top partner level:

Industry	Hard Worker	Delusion
Publishing	New Writers	Published, Make $
Insurance	New Agents	Annuity from clients
Innovator	Inventors	Patents not honored
Investors	Entrepreneur	Rich and owner
Partner Firm	CPA, lawyer, etc.	Reach partner
Sales	Rep	Keep/serve customers

The goal of those who want to trap others is to hire a lot of new people who bring in new customers. After acquiring customers, reduce the number of these past new hires and replace them with new new hires that bring in new customers. These can be modern day sweat shops devoid of spirituality where the money flows to the owners. The owners keep the dream in front of the workers to keep them working with the hope of getting joy in the long term future. If you complain, then you are not part of the delusional future anymore and no longer will work there.

So what are your options? It really is pretty simple:

1) Play in their sand box and use their infrastructure; and leave when you are ready "to go own your own experidigm".

2) Build your own assets (i.e. intellectual property, etc.) and sign deals with your customers and build your team to deliver.

3) Create your NEXT experidigm.

4) Improve the education system.

Always create your experidigm.

Negativity with Limiting Beliefs

Frankly, when pointing and looking up at the positive experidigm, the invented negativity of the willful "you are..." is like roaches scurrying around on the ground at your feet, trying to get you to pay attention to them. The roaches have lots of motion with nothing really happening. All the roaches do the same thing, just like every 'you are..." spouts negativity and judgment. If "I am..." pays attention to the negativity, the negativity starts to come alive and push down the "I am...." Otherwise, negativity is the delusion created by "you are...." The "I am..." does not create negativity.

Some might say that pain comes into an "I am ..." life, like the death of a loved one or financial failure, and this is negative. This is pain, and pain is fleeting and goes away. A person can turn pain into suffering, and carry this suffering around with them as an excuse to stay in pain. Suffering is negative. Any excuse tends to keep a person in the "you are…" suffering state. The way out of negativity is to point to an experidigm, and focus on that with your connected "I am…" team.

Some will say negativity is a "fact" and an observation. No, if it creates limiting beliefs in the "I am…," it is a delusional belief. Stop believing in negativity and get rid of it. Point up. Negativity is a "you are…" wanting to extend their invented problem and Taker cycle to enslave "I am…s." Negativity is an invented problem.

Driving

Although I use a "Path of Life" analogy to show a continuous journey to the Infinite, our life is not constrained by any path, road, goal or direction we can conceive of unless we want and will it to be that way. The point of the Path was to say that we move toward the Infinite, and along with the movement we must deflect and avoid certain unconnected people. We are not driving to any destination or goal. Driving is too limiting and controlling. We are living our willful creation, and if we make that driving, then it is driving, or if we make living that flowing from one experidigm to another, we truly live free to create. Have the "I am..." flow with you as you create your experiences.

Driving feels safe and secure, like we are in control of the external world. Feeling safe and secure is just like building a wall because of the delusion fear. We build walls to keep fear and its' minions out. Safety and security are the flipside delusions of fear that keep you on a constraining Path.

The End

The "end" sounds so final. Well, it is. Your space suit will stop operating one day and will not return. It is like throwing away a pair of old clothes. You will never use those clothes again. I do not feel sad when I throw away a pair of old clothes because I am happy I have a new choice to make--what new clothes will I wear?

Your "I am..." is your "I am...." It will always be your "I am...." Hopefully you are connected to all "I am...s" and the Infinite "I am...." Can you imagine a new space suit not in the human form? Our minds are normally so limited by our senses, we have a hard time imagining much beyond our earthly existence. Let's wish for access to our own Hubble telescope to view the infinite, and we could expand more. Even better, we are already connected to the infinite, and from our infinite perspective, in some future times, we can view our new space suit selection from the infinite perspective of choice. I think I better practice making choices so my "I am..." does a good job selecting then.

PART 9:

Evolving

Resurrect Experidimging

I bet when you read that word "resurrect" it creates strong feelings in you. Positive in the sense that newness can be recreated, and a new vigor can be created and lived. Negative in the sense of disbelief that a living thing can be brought back to life. In both emotions we focus on life, and life taking on a new vigor.

New vigor is the natural flow of the infinite evolving and changing experiences and all connections with those experiences. Resurrection happens around us all the time. Our space suit and our associated senses cannot measure it or know it. We are not in control of it, but we are participating in it all the time if we are connected. The act of creation is an act of resurrection. Our "I am..." knows that resurrection is happening all around us.

It is natural for our "I am..." to receive the gifts of all the resurrections and creations around us. For us to participate in that, even in the small way that our space suit enables us, is joy.

To deny our creative ability is to deny our link with the Infinite and the connection to all the resurrections. To deny the ability to create a joyful experience is to deny the presence of your connected "I am..." free will.

Change and evolution are natural manifestations of resurrection. We will discuss these further as they relate to our space suits

The real question about resurrection is not that it happens, but what type of resurrections occur, and can I become part of them and for how long? This is a different thought than the cycle of life, which as we see, is based on the planet cycles we observe with our senses. We have been creating stories of these cycles with every human culture. The reality is that these cycles would surely be different if we were on a different planet and a different universe, so they are not part of our "I am...." Therefore, can resurrection happen for our "I am...?"

Here is a thought -- creative things propagate and destructive things destroy. Creative things connect and grow; destructive things destroy. If I had to bet, I would bet creative things evolve, change, and resurrect in an infinite number of ways and forms.

Creativity resurrects. Infinite creativity is enormous. Infinite creativity is like walking through a museum and looking at all the styles, absorbing them and choosing them for your experidigm at the appropriate time. The museum just waits for you and stretches on and on and never ends. Infinite creativity is like being on a tour that just keeps going to new places with so many layers including history and culture. Infinite creativity is like looking up at the night sky and knowing that each star supports worlds, and there are more worlds than can be counted in a lifetime. Infinite creativity is looking over the horizon and seeing that it goes on forever. Infinite creativity is part of experidigm resurrection. The "I am..." resurrects in the Infinite "I am...."

Everything Evolves

From the point of view looking out at today, everything looks fairly similar as it did yesterday. All the things and processes around continue in a similar fashion, changing ever so slightly, just as my breathing does, but we do not really notice. We get caught up in our individual rhythm of life. Then we name the rhythm so we can add some permanence to it: like day, nights, work, eating, driving, etc.

Rhythm just does not exist without our "I am…" flow to create and connect it. Your "I am…" gives rhythm to your space suit, your breathing and your senses. Our rhythm integrates how we evolve in a coordinated and seamless fashion. Rhythm synchronizes our flows and is unique to each of us. Rhythm is beyond music and part of our evolution flow, just as love is part of our "I am…" connection.

Ok, so you are thinking that a "you are…" person creates their rhythm. No, they take another's' "I am…" rhythm and use it in their Taker cycle. A "you are…" still has some "I am…" while they are alive, but it is locked in their self-imposed prison. A "you are…" can stop their "you are…" at any time and liberate their "I am…" from their self-imposed prison.

Joy ebbs and flows. Joy flows along S-curves as discussed in Part 2. Like anything that flows, Joy has a rhythm, sometimes strong, sometimes weak, sometimes fast, and sometimes lingering. The rhythm plays out as we layer experidigms on top of each other

The more experidigms, the more flow and the more joy. Our rhythm changes when our flow changes. When we create and will a new experidigm, a faster tempo and rhythm is set. Our rhythm changes with the seasons of our lives. Sometimes fast as a youth and slower as we age. If one develops a fast rhythm later in life, a feeling of youth comes over our mind although the body may say something else -- ouch.

It can be hard to evolve as an individual, all alone setting the rhythm. In a competitive world, an issue is that the winner is still all alone. To evolve, the question is how to do it – either by cooperation or competition? With cooperation, one is rarely alone.

Everything Changes

Change gets a bad reputation from "you are..." people. 'You are..." people do not want to see change because they want to keep their problem the focus for givers and take from those working on their problem. They want to control change and givers. "You are..." people want others to believe that pain comes from change, so they encourage and demand that change be avoided. Ask yourself, why do people not help you with important changes in your life? Change frees people from stagnation and problems. Change requires that we experience and connect to feel fresh joy.

Change is not the enemy. Change is the essence of the "I am..." energy. Change means that flow happens and that stagnation is overcome. When is stagnation good? Never.

Those who create exist in evolution, change and resurrection as their "I am..." flow.

Here is an interesting thought…which has caused more space suits to stop operating: change, which is nonjudgmental and flows only one way toward the creative new, or "you are..." people who want to stay in control?

If you want to have a joyful "I am…" in your space suit, you should welcome change and deflect TTers and Takers.

Change is natural and is always occurring with everything, no matter what people try to do to stop it. Some call change entropy and chaos. That is natural, when no planning is involved. Or, there is willful change based on our picture of the experidigm future. When action starts toward the experidigm, both natural chaotic change and willful change combine and have a constantly changing interplay and rhythm. Control is lost when natural change takes over. Or is it? Or did one ever really have control? Maybe all this space suit has is to point in a direction, and act and do.

Sometimes, striving for efficiency and effectiveness just takes change completely out of the process. This might sound good, and it could be for a while, but change has been going on outside and all around the efficient and effective process, which might make the process irrelevant and obsolete. Then, when noticing the process is no longer efficient and valid, a new experidigm must be created in a rapid change process. Even if change is kept out of the process, change will jump back in with full destructive fury. Change is always working.

When handling change, the perspective can be either from an individual (i.e. stagnant) or group (status quo) viewpoint. The initial viewpoint of each is normally to stamp change out, to live in the security and delusion of control and change elimination. The best way to move forward with change is cooperation and working with the change process and many "I am…s" in that change process. However, some use competition to push change, which can be good, but competition can slip into "you are…" and "to the winner goes the spoils," which might limit cooperation. The lust and pride of winning can overpower community and cooperation.

Just Picture and Do

Enabling joy is just not that hard. Just picture a simple experidigm and act. Learn and connect to make joy happen. If success has occurred in the past, then success seems easier, and one can predict success. Achieve the first simple success, change the picture, and get another success -- smiling is a first sign of success.

Of course, bad things happen; bad people hurt others, but bad things are just not part of the experidigm. Bad hurts, but bad has nothing to do with the experidigm. Focusing on the experidigm assists in deflecting, avoiding and just eliminating any bad thing. Focus on joy using discipline and the "I am…" connection.

No reasons to over think and over plan any aspect of the experidigm. Just get stated, do, and learn. Over thinking and over planning tend to build in frustration because the thinking and planning might not become the reality. Then striving to make the plans reality only starts to make matters worse with frustration building. We do not have things or get things, we experience them. In that experience, we have joy in the flow. In that experience one learns how the experience works and can be enhanced for joy. In an average life we might have over 91,250 experiences (i.e. 5 experiences per day for 50 years times 365). We have many experiences in life to practice with and learn how to make an experidigm. If one is dedicated to "I am…ing" and joy, one can have double the experiences.

Of course, if bad things happen, the bad things will not keep us from the 91,250 experiences. The only thing that can really stop a person from these experiences is that a person will allow being stopped and allow the "you are…" to suppress their "I am…."

Others have said to focus on NOW and live in the NOW to reduce life's frustrations, especially the risk of not capturing your goal. This is wrong and creates aimlessness and joyless wandering. Of course the NOW is imperfect and transitory, but the NOW must be focused on the "I am…" and what to point toward. The focus on the "I am…" NOW is to <u>do</u> and <u>point</u> to the experidigm created and designed by infinite "I am…ness." NOW is where learning happens by doing, and what NEXT might be good to do. Learning occurs because there is a direction to the doing. The direction may not be perfect, but it is evolving through learning to get to the current experidigm and then declare NEXT, to go to the NEXT "I am…" growth.

Unfortunately, learning includes both good and bad. Sure, joy is good. Could some "bad" be joy in disguise? Doing is the cause which brings the manifestation of the effect and the learning (from the effect being different than the designed experidigm). Sometimes pain, suffering, failure, hurt, disillusionment, and tribulation come after (and sometimes before) doing. Many religions claim that suffering enables learning and forces a good hard look at the "I am…" and then redirection of the experidigm. If suffering manifests, the time is NOW to declare NEXT, and create a new experidigm and get new connections. Expand the "I am…" by connecting with other "I am…s." Doing the NEXT experidigm is important to leave bad behind as only a memory. We can lose this memory latter after we learn. It's so important to learn how to say NEXT, and do it.

Living in the NOW with no focused direction forward related to an "I am…" experidigm is dangerous. With only a NOW (and no experidigm) focus, an "I am…" is highly susceptible to falling into the status quo of Turd Throwers or getting trapped in a Taker cycle. With no experidigm to focus and guide, the constant marketing bombardment of the day begins to manipulate choice and create the feeling of belonging to the ad and their message, losing the "I am…" to the "you are…" message. To avoid getting lost in the NOW, focus on pointing and acting directed toward the experidigm so others can understand, follow and participate.

Taking the space suit analogy a step further reveals how we should explore and experience life in our space suits. An astronaut puts on their suit and gets into the spaceship and takes off to explore outer space. The space suit allows the person to withstand the bad and lifeless environment and explore using their senses. But the astronaut really does not just want to stay in the spaceship capsule, they want to walk on the new surface like the moon. The spaceship capsule is just the thing to take them there and the space suit allows them to walk around and explore the new surface or to just float in space. The spaceship is like the status quo. We can get so comfortable in the spaceship status quo that we do not want to leave it and explore other experiences. We just stay locked in the spaceship in the space suit. That is terrible and no way to live life. Picture an experidigm and use your "I am…" and your space suit to explore the infinite.

Common Delusions:

+   Ego exists--- is a delusion.

The Ego does not exist, nor do the Id and Superego (for definitions see reference 5). Like any classification, they try to define and summarize what is observed in the space suit world. What happens in the space suit world are experiences and connections, and classifying them only serves the purposes of the "you are…." As we make chooses for our connections and experiences, we hopefully use the creativity of our connected "I am…," and we create our experiences outside of the problem world of Takers and TTers.

+   Evil exists--- is a delusion.

Evil does not exist and cannot recreate itself. Free will creates "you are..." and "you are..." appears to be evil as it takes. Taking is a willful act outside the connections of the 'I am...' and exists only in the space suit world.

Here is an interesting thought: Accepting evil as real is just another "you are..." problem created 1) to control "I am..." givers, and 2) as an excuse to allow "You are..." to be hurtful – "the devil made me do it!"

+   Goals are helpful to plan a life – goals constrain the creativity of life.

There is a dichotomy between goals and experiencing life. Goals may help when doing coordinated actions in business (like budgeting, like launching a product, etc.). Goals fail miserably when applied to experiencing life. Here is why —life is the connected gift of the Infinite to be experienced in the infinite fullness and joy of Infinite. The infiniteness cannot be planned or controlled in any way. So trying to put goals on the Infinite is like trying to swim across the ocean – quickly you go to Plan B and change your goals and let the Infinite set your sails.

+   Expectations are a form of goals. Setting expectations does the same things that setting goals does for a life. They constrain a life. Having false expectations can be a starting point of a problem that a Taker uses to enslave your "I am...."

APPENDIX:
Reality Starts Here

Epilogue

The feeling of the experidigm always remains and always flows upward in the infinite. The feeling reappears and renews in a new context and points upward for more creating and more experidigms.

Just as a poem is surrounded by music and a lingering feeling, life is surrounded by joy and a lingering experidigm. Words appear to make the poem, yet words are not the lingering feeling; a wholeness is. Life is not to be understood, it is to be collected through experiences. Understanding and defining the words, the parts, the innovation, the method, the success, material possessions, or anything can distract from the lingering joy experience. Understanding and defining is not life. Nurturing the "I am…" to prosper and deflecting the "you are…" allows joy to flourish.

The space suit is confined. Experidigm memories are not confined. Memories flow and grow. "I am…" is unbounded and belongs with experidigms.

The Joy equation pushes distractions aside and allows focus on experidigms and connections, leading to joy. Learning how to experidigm and how to connect can be taught. Experidigms evolve, combine, and birth more experidigms, spinning off joy during the flow of action.

The economic evolution to selling holistic experiences from the current selling of parts and pieces creates an economic system where value and excess profit are related to all participants of the experidigm, not just to product or capital owners. Experidigms flourish.

Spirituality Choice

Everything is connected. Everything shares atoms, energy, life, and spirit. Atoms, energy, life and spirit make up our space suit and all exist whether our space suit is here or not. All respond to intention and the will of the Infinite. Whether that response is automatic from a predetermined physical state law like gravity or intentional depends on the flow, direction, and context. What flows is atoms, energy, life spirit, spirit-related love, joy, and goodness. What creates flow and its components is the Infinite, the one, the God. Everyone can choose to be at one with the Infinite – to create and connect and experience the Joy equation. Of course, anyone can choose to be disconnected and be a taker and take to survive. What do you choose - joy or taking?

History by "you are..." Takers

The quick answer is that many ancient and current histories are being written by the "you are..." taker-winners, and those "you are..." stories support the TTer and Taker mantra. The bottom line delusion created is that it is easier to take and manipulate using "you are...." We are the winners, so be like us.

Early in our lives we are almost perfect "I am..." soaking in all our experiences and using all our senses. Hopefully, you were raised in an "I am..." connected family and have been exposed to the Joy equation and importance of connections and experiences. If not, you will learn "you are..." early, as society and religion send their "you are..." distractions. As we grow, we are introduced to the society and religious community norms and they encourage us to act in a certain way and focus us on their acceptable future. When you let this in, you can become them, the status quo, and maybe totally subject your "I am..." to their will. This group "you are..." will can lead to all kinds of taking. Let's take a quick look at history on how the "you are..." impacts history and what we know.

The family is a starting point for most people. The "I am..." is exposed to physical nurturing and culture expectations. The "I am..." begins to let in what other people say and do. "Reality" of the external world is subject to the interpretation of family members. Familial settings like meals together repeat and we get in a rhythm. The family talks of values, supplies the basic necessities of life, and creates a hierarchy (a family pecking order) the individual must fit into. Notions of love, caring, and God are being formed. The "I am..." starts wondering about what the future holds, but few people actually talk about or assist in picturing a future. Perhaps no end in mind, except the traditional be a doctor or a lawyer.

Many families collaborate to build a community that shares infrastructure--roads, services, etc. People live together and grow a community together, and the community makes rules and laws so peace and order is maintained. As time progresses, most community people accept norms and live in a similar way and see the world in a similar way. Individuals find their role in this community or search elsewhere.

Eventually the community builds excess value and accumulates wealth and has a surplus of material things and infrastructure. With an excess, the community initiates ways to protect and keep the wealth for itself, and makes laws to ensure it can keep the wealth. The consciousness begins to shift from creative "I am..." to "you are..." taking. Soon armies are created to defend the wealth and walls are built to protect from those outside the community who might take the wealth. Deeper and deeper the consciousness focuses on what the community has, not necessarily on what will be and on future experidigms. The goal is to lock in the status quo. Walls tend to lock things either in or out and subjugate free "I am..." will.

Walls and wars go hand and hand. War is a method for takers to take because they choose to be unconnected and unable to create, so only taking is left for them. Taking and war are the delusion created when the "I am..." is in prison, and no creative experidigm, except talking war can be created by a "you are...." The war world only exists in a taker world, not a love "I am..." connected and sharing world. It builds on itself as it tells "you are..." stories of conquest and defeat. History books focus on telling this "you are..." victory story and keep justifying the right to take, versus the right to joy and experidigms. War is not natural; it is a tool of the taker cycle. For example, create a problem and enslave everyone into fixing it. We create an enemy problem and we must unite to fight against this problem. War is invented.

The Infinite will flow and connect whether we have wars are not. Joy will come to me only if "I am..." connected and experience joy, while deflecting TTers. Life will continue to flow. The real question is do I want to be part of that experience flow, or will I let others take me and define me?

Examples of "you are..."

Everyone is familiar with a "you are…," as the latter have infiltrated every aspect of life. The world is bombarded by "you are…" mentality everywhere. The vast majority of "I am…ers" are not taught how to deflect these TTers (except with the book *Soaring to Awesome – Turd Throwers Beware*) and thus develop counter strategies in an ad hoc, as-needed fashion. Many thusly learn to "fight fire with fire", and degrade into a "you are…" as they spout "you are…" arguments back at the original "you are…." Fighting fire with fire simply creates more fire and more "you are…s," and less and less "I am…s." Instead, use the TTer shield to deflect the "you are…" and state your "I am…" (and a "you are…" might follow your example and become an "I am..." again). Here are some short and simple examples where one experiences "you are..." in life:

+ Political debates and interviews and related TV and radio political talk shows:

Many times, the winner of the debate is the person who can successfully redefine his or her opponent as the "you are..." branding statement used in the debate. A common example is "you are a liar", which then casts doubt on anything else the person says. A common tactic is to define the opponent as part of a hated group: "you are a communist," "you are a racist," "you voted against women," etc.—this list can go on forever. The bottom line is to deflect the statement and restate who "I am...: again and again.

Many times in political interviews, the interviewer asks questions to brand the politician in their "you are..." light. For example, "some claim you are a bully?" The wrong reply, "I am not a bully". The right answer, "I am...." Another example, "Did you vote against Mexicans?" The wrong answer – "No". The only answer is to state the "I am..." and what the "I am..." stands for on the subject being discussed.

+ High School "you are..." bullies:

Few things are more stressful than a "you are..." attack at school by a single person or a group of bullies. The attacks all seem similar. The bully TTers single the victim out and all say disgusting verbal things to define the person as worthless or bad or evil. There is no real purpose except for dominance and control, and that the TTers want to take the "I am..." away.

Example as a school girl victim – a group of girls walk up to the victim and say:

"You are a slut"
"You are ugly"
"You are fat"

"We hate you"

And then some guys walk up and say "you are a slut". And they all follow up with this TTing on texting and social media. The abuse continues.

Example as a school boy victim – You are drawing a cartoon picture and then four athletes ("jocks") grab the picture and rip it up and spill your drink on you, saying:

"You are a geek"
"You kiss your mom"
"You love boys"
"You are a loser"

Once again, they all follow up with this TTing by texting and social media. The abuse continues.

Read my books on how to *Avoid Takers* and to deflect *Turd Throwers*.

+   Family "you are…" indoctrination:

Family life is not always perfect. Some families are not supportive of individual family members and their "I am…." Similar to High School, some parents attack the "I am…" of their children and take the children's' "I am…" away by saying:

"You are so stupid"
"You are a failure"
"You are worthless"
"You are a loser"
"You have no…ability…talent…"

The attack can last until the children leave the house.

+   Friends and Lovers attack the "I am…" in arguments:

Everyone has witnessed or been part of a heated argument between angry friends or lovers. In many of these cases, the "You are…" phrases fly back and forth to hurt each other – and they do hurt the "I am…" of each other.

"You are cheating…" --- "You are liar…"
"You make me sick…" --- "You are sad and so stupid…"

Many more "you are…s" will flow and continue. Then the next morning each victim feels like the new definition of 'you are…'. A week later this 'you are…' repeats itself. A year later each party becomes a "you are…." The "I am…" can get lost. Maybe that is why the divorce rate is so high.

+   Performance review "you are…" and being redefined:

The work context of performance reviews occurs every six months or once per year when employees meet with the boss and go through a formal discussion on achievements versus goals. This sounds good and can assist in making performance better aligned with goals and make needed improvements. Making improvements together is good. However, reviews can become very "you are…" personal, and these you are statements can be very similar to the "you are…" statement in a lover's quarrel, but without the loud voice yelling. For example, the boss might say:

"You are stupid"
"You are a liar"
"You are lazy"

And the list can go on and on. Then, the boss summarizes the "you are…" statements that the employee must become. The employee loses their "I am…" at work. The situation did not have to degrade into a "you are…." The situation should focus on goals and how to achieve them, and not a defining "you are…" note.

+   The manipulation of "you are…" ads:

Marketing ads try to paint a picture of you as someone who is better by using their product. The ad's intent is to manipulate you to be their "you are...." There are so many examples. A simple one is "Open Happiness" as you drink sugar water, like drinking sugar water leads to happiness - no, it leads to diabetes. So "you are happy" drinking sugar water.

Ads that say "you are..." are very effective at grabbing the "I am..." and redefining it to the "you are...."

+ The angry service provider argument:

Disagreements can take an either/or path. Either both parties say their "I am..." point of view, or one/both parties go down the route of "you are..." redefining. Public arguments in the workplace can go down the "you are..." path in almost any setting, including when a customer is serviced. The service provider or the customer can go down the "you are..." path:

"Are you stupid?"
"Are you a fool?"
"Are you deaf?"
"You are wrong"
"You are rude"

Either side of the argument can say each of these.

The list of "you are..." examples could be the length of another book.

Examples of "I am..." Biographies

Here are a sampling of biographies of those who live a life of seeing experidigms, enlisting others in their connections, and creating and doing toward joy, and then evolving to their NEXT transition and experidigm. Moving through transitions and evolving are part of the flow and joy of life.

+ Robert – Learning and Doing

Summary: At first life was about learning and doing, the perfect partnership. Then life grew in to expressing my ego while establishing my boundaries with the right packaging (dressing nice) and displaying the symbols of success to gain acceptance. All while raising loving, exceptional children. At the end of day it was about either surviving or finding the next distraction. Now it is all about "being" who I am, from being to doing, from achieving to appreciating, from planning and plotting to trusting and banishing fear, and now living in the experience and creating the life I desire…my Experidigm.

Surviving and Finding Distraction

Bob was not supposed to do the things he has successfully accomplished in the work and social worlds. Mostly, he was the unique one who looked different and was not exactly allowed to be part of the club. He is a black man who in 1970 to 1990 prospered and survived in the WASP (white, Anglo-Saxon, protestant) working world. He learned to live in two worlds - one black, one white. He really did not pay attention to his obvious difference. He was a victim, but never thought of being victimized. He read, he learned, he grew, and he brushed off rejection, found sponsors and supporters at each level and moved on. His reading as a child revealed a world beyond and showed him examples of those who lived a different world. He believed he could do anything he wanted. He would roll up his sleeves, get involved, ask what and why questions until others got frustrated, learned, and delivered the results with a smile, and kept moving forward. He saw his next steps and moves to the next Experidigm, and was always living his next experience vision in the present.

For most of his business career, he did it for the experience of doing, achieving, and the joy of solving business problems from which others shied away. He sought not the money, but the experience of something new. He could transition to new industries and new playgrounds to acquire new experiences. Bob always moved forward and upward.

He was able to lead new "doing" in large emerging industries: consumer products, cable television, the Internet, e-commerce, pay-per-view and video-on-demand services, and technology entrepreneurial startups. In each, he rapidly progressed to the next experience as a new business executive faster than most. Today, the leaders of these industries acknowledge his energy, ability to deliver, and smiling kindness. They respect him. They count on him. They smile, happily.

He is rich with memories but not rich in the monetary trophies of success. He was penalized by racism in all its forms and exclusions: in the extended family, in society, and at work. Expectations from the family were high, and rarely contained positive reinforcement and led to a problem with bad stuttering (which was later corrected with hard work, understanding and the help of a mentor boss). Other's alcoholism distracted energy and time. In society, others tried to redefine him—"you should be a laborer, not an architect because that is what your people do; or, you are not smart enough." At work, he always quickly moved through and up in organizational responsibility, but the money and prestige did not follow or match his peers. He feels, "people may make me a victim, but I will keep going and doing. I choose not to be victimized." Instead, he avoided and deflected abusive people while he took advantage of his strengths to create his next transition – "I read, asked questions, solved problems by doing, and happily socialized and networked, then moved on".

Experience, Wisdom, Choices

The order of his major professional transitions is shown below. In each, he learned his craft, and he got major things done, while others were stuck. In each, there was some "cognitive dissidence" about achievement, doing good, but not receiving acceptance, and getting the manipulative push of others to do better (so they get). He always wanted to please by doing. He always wanted to work within the business of advertising and the television business. The people seemed smart, educated, and somewhat elitist.

- Executive, Visual Talking-ads in communication

- Co-Founder, President, COO, New Urban
  Entertainment Television

- President, Bell Atlantic Video Services-subscription model and
  selling local advertising

- Senior Vice President, Home Shopping Network-ads and selling
  on TV

- Vice President, New York Times Cable Television

- Vice President, Citicorp, Bankcard Marketing

- Group Product Director, Johnson & Johnson-
  Product Management

- Account Management, BBD&O-entry level to the advertising business

- Lever Brothers and Charles Pfizer- Field sales and Key
  Account Management.

His biggest transitions were:

1) Breaking away from the family and defining himself.

2) Getting a first rate education and devising his own model for
   learning at Howard University while being surrounded by individuals like himself. Exposed to a classical education and leaders
   in their own right, learning to think and defining his own personal experience.

3) Knowing that he could do what he envisioned. He saw himself in
   the world of television and how to get there.

Being successful in all the business transitions tended to reinforce the
delusional trappings of success. The fancy dressing, nice meals, and all the

other material things "success" brings can be distracting and keep one in a numb, false state of happiness. Then, life happens, changes, and forces one to open his eyes and reevaluate, and point to a new transition. As his work and family failed around him, the "why" questioning continued and brought a closer and closer understanding of self-respect (I AM), and to trust everything will work out and that spirituality can fill the void in anyone's life. His "being" is more important than his doing. His thoughts on "being" come true and guide the doing.

The many obstacles he saw and experienced (i.e. racism, stuttering, alcoholism, etc.) appear as though they are still there, but they have nothing to do with his being. They do not exist in that being. What exists is the joy to create his being in any transformative way he chooses. He still knows he can do anything, but it is different now. He still has the same core skills, a bit more enhanced, but it is different now. It really is different now. He is connected to his being; he is always seeing the "good" with a smile. He said, "The bigger the problem, the closer I get to God. I grow with God.

He is so thankful for having learned how to grow and transition to his visualizations. His gratitude list:

- Living a fulfilling life.

- Achieved all the things he envisioned and set out to achieve.

- Raised a family of which he can be proud of. Children he knows who love him.

- Kept marriage intact; something that took a great effort.

- Not only became a vice president of a Fortune 500 Company, but a divisional president of another.

- Saw other parts of the world.

- Has a number of caring friends and admirers.

- Regained health, a 25-year cancer and diabetes survivor.

- Took a risk, started a business and survived.

- Found an accepting a Higher Power and a Loving God.

I Am

He smiles every day, often as a metaphysician. You may have met him. He is the guy you see reading, or the person who keeps asking "what and why," or the guy who politely gets it done. He is the guy who happily sees it and does it. He is everywhere, not really seen, blending into the joy of life.

+ Dave – Engineer Innovator

Summary: Life changing innovation happens and through this I have learned to be fearless. I innovate and jump into the innovation abyss and so far have always come out better, smiling. I say bring on change. I have learned the innovation and change abyss does not hurt, but fearing the abyss hurts more and creates even bigger problems. Never underestimate personal strength and value, using them to experience life and overpower the abyss fear. My successful life transitions are: lost to known, finding fellow innovators, sadly experiencing everyone not engaged, jumping to the next business, and focusing on having fun in specific areas.

As a child, Dave dreamed of being an engineer inventor; creating the new and pioneering. He played with construction toys. His family was not aspirational, and he was brought up in a relatively poor area lacking opportunities for work. Like so many kids, he staggered through early school in a boyish sort of way not knowing what he wanted to do. His first try at college was not productive, but he learned to stay away from school subjects he found no value in like higher math. With school on temporary hold, he was lucky getting a high paying job in a tin mine. This transition was to kick start the dream forward.

It turns out mines require all sorts of engineering skills because they are often remote islands of industry requiring one to be a "jack of all engineering trades." In a short time, Dave was learning all sorts of engineering, applying it creatively, and he loved it, even travelling to South and West Africa. A greater love than mining, his soon-to-be wife agreed with Dave to be one together in England, so he left behind mining to find more innovation and engineering. Marriage and having a family with two children added stability, a nurturing environment, and a place to sink one's roots.

With stability at home, Dave took a leap and joined the Research and Development facility of a global industrial gases company. This was a playground for innovation because every industry uses industrial gases like nitrogen and oxygen, so the team focused on every industry. Here, he co-created with other innovators and received many patents reaching his childhood dream of being an engineer inventor. Part of this experience was the realization of just how difficult it is to take an idea from concept to fruition and commercialization. Innovations are like children; they require nurturing and care to grow, and once grown, must stand on their own feet to succeed or fail. A tough lesson for a 'parent' to experience.

Seeing that innovation failure is most easily caused by poorly engaged people or even the foibles of management is disappointing. Innovation is fraught with many pitfalls. To avoid the pitfalls, ask lots of questions, work smart, and work well with others. Dave worked in the USA launching products and then back to Europe to manage a global business. The main way to success in these products and businesses was networking by staying in contact with experts and customers. When the parent company was being acquired, Dave took a retirement parachute which has enabled him to focus on a more innovative and riskier career.

The entrepreneurial transition was driven by big company frustration and avoiding the politics that cause being bogged down. Dave joined the leadership of a young, start-up company and launched new technology leveraging Dave's love of engineering. "The roller-coaster of a start-up is both terrifying and exhilarating at the same time." After several years of success and innovation, like all roller-coaster rides, there is a time to get off and go to a different ride.

Instead of joining another company, Dave created his own advisory firm, and, as a consultant, supports companies needing transitions related to innovation. The companies range from mammoth utilities to ideas looking for a start-up. Clients need that special rare enthusiasm and knowledge of how to turn ideas into commercial products. Most think innovation is like jumping off a cliff into an abyss and they fear how far they will fall. The reality is that for great ideas the fall is never that far; the real challenge is to jump intelligently. The real danger is giving into a fearful imagination. Dave's transitional experiences demonstrated to him that the abyss can not only be managed but engineered successfully. In fact, Dave has realized there is no abyss if you maintain your vision; keep pointing up to the goal experience, focus on reaching it, then point to the next goal experience, and repeat.

+   Mark - Planning

Summary: Why was I dealt this struggling, daily grind of a young life? My teenage understanding – I have choice, I have the ability to envision and plan my future and the continuing desire to grab my dream. My life will change for the better. Working through college, passing the CPA exam, and learning how to respect work relationships, I kept my "eye on the prize" of being a caring corporate executive and a loving father. At every decision crossroad, I reinforced my burning desire to be better than I am now, always asking how and adjusting to do better. Sure, frustrations crept in challenging expectations and plans, but desire to continue and participate was stronger. Everyone can choose better, become better, get ahead and stand together with group success and personal freedom.

"I am extremely optimistic." Mark sees the future positively happening as a plan unfolding making adjustments when necessary, and everybody getting ahead. Not necessarily easy, but he was always determined. His philosophy was sharpened and crystallized at 15 years old after his mother passed away leaving nine children in a tough blue collar life. Mom said "you have gifts, so use them." First, was to secure the financial survival of the family, so Mark went to work while learning at high school. Life was difficult. A plan was needed.

Mark knew that just working long hours was not the complete answer. He hung with smart kids and stimulated his intellect. The first plan was to excel at university education and then have an executive professional career. Seeing the plan unfold every day in his mind made the full-time job as a clerk and janitor working from midnight to 8am doable and worth it. Working in freezing cold was somehow OK when pointing to such a good future. The plan also contained a wonderful wife and kids.

Picture the power of a plan to carry one though a physical and grueling 8 hour work day, followed by a full day learning at high school all the way through college. This builds discipline and strengthens desire. College graduation marked the first step in the plan. Next, Mark married his high school sweetheart and 50 years later are still going strong together. The plan said he needed more learning so on to graduate business school getting an MBA and passing the CPA exam in the first sitting. The plan is being fulfilled and enters the NEXT phase – building an executive career. While at graduate school, Mark is recruited by the largest company in the world and begins his career.

Which life are we really living? The daily one thrown at us or the one we plan will happen. For those who have a plan, both lives are lived, and the life flows toward the plan. For those who have no plan, only the daily grind is lived and little flow of life happens. Get a plan. Get an Experidigm.

Working at one of the world's largest oil companies, he quickly rose in the ranks and became an executive, moving into a new position every three years. Each job transition was to a completely different operating group with all new people. The plan keeps improving with each transition, growing the burning desire "to get better than I am now." Like his mother said, "you have gifts, so use them", and learning and doing was a key gift. Sharing the gifts was part of that gift. Sharing includes being a mentor, recruiting and developing others to assist them with their plan(s). Mark led thousands. Smile when the plan evolves and comes true and grows to something else that is good. Mark believes all who use their gifts (with a plan) get ahead. We all stand on the shoulders of those who have led the way before, and we do the same for those who follow. Have confidence to improve your gifts and use that confidence to assist others do well. Sometimes, for those wasting their talent, a wakeup call needs to be delivered, to get them on their plan, and to be responsible for their plan and moving on their way to developing their gifts. Delivering a wakeup call requires tact, and we all need to do that well. The key is to deliver the wakeup call and care to get others moving.

The plan is never perfect. In a 36 year career as an executive with a new job every three years or so, adjustments will need to be made. No one gets each management position they want when they feel they should have it. Only a few get to the top spot because there are only a few top spots – it is simple math. Frustration, rejection, anger and other emotions may try to take control of the plan, but fight back with a positive attitude. Realize the fabulous future still exists but the parameters have just changed some. Keep pushing, keep adjusting, keep applying, and keep sharing the gifts. Being intellectually stimulated adds energy and wisdom to adjusting the plan, and a smile adds the necessary care. No room for jealousy as others have earned their futures as well.

Here are Mark's major professional transitions at work:

- Upstream General Auditor

- General Auditor - Chemical and Corporate Services

- Global Inter-Company Accounting Manager

- Controller, Pipeline Company

- U.S. Supply and Marketing Accounting Manager

- Latin America Chemical Business Services Manager

- U.S. Downstream Financial Coordinator

- Audit Manager - Operations in Australia

Looking back at all the joy and the few moments of sadness, the plan created a good life. Mark rose above early resource limitations and found education and learning did indeed enable a 36 year executive career with many, many job transitions. The idea of a plan was passed on to Mark's two children who also graduated college and pursue their different careers around the world. The idea of a plan was shared with so many others at work and at universities who got better and adjusted their plans and kept pushing on, sharing their gifts.

"I am extremely optimistic" about the future. "Todays' technologies, especially information and connection technology allow more and more people to live a life on their plan." Mark points to the success of the grandchildren and their future plans. Promoting university scholarship continues the intellectual learning.

+ Dave – Point Up

Summary: Life presents moments of decision. Wake up, grab them, jump on board, use creative energy, and join and lead others to move. When life situations keep expecting and taking, get free and get better, learn and go. Be the first; keep climbing, chose a better life, smiling all the way. Sure, some ways prove wrong, then change direction and smile. I have decided to lovingly break free and expand from my birth family, from increasing school levels, from defining jobs, and lead my life at home, at work and wherever I am.

Sometimes the positive foundation of a family is absent. Sometimes the family creates a trapped, draining experience. Dave broke free from a controlling family by having the court system grant him a foster care family. With a stable roof over his head, he could attend college, being the first in his family. Learning is key to making plans and dreams come true. He focused on subjects like welding, architecture, and computer-aided design. At college career day, a construction supply company offered Dave a job to use his new skills.

On the job, Dave focused and performed well in positions of increasing responsibility and became a subject matter expert for specific products. With this learning and improvement also came knowledge of how to improve bad life habits that were heavy baggage brought from an under privileged and abusive upbringing. Sobriety was the goal and fully achieved through the grace of the Infinite.

Setting a goal for higher responsibility, Dave transitioned from a technical career to a sales career and learned how to work with customers and the internal organization to deliver. Dave built better communication skills and practiced how to be a leader and positively impact and enable others. Each bit of progress and learning led to the desire for more learning and more progress. Dave viewed getting an MBA as allowing him to be a well-rounded businessman able to run a company. He worked full-time and built a family of two children in the five years it took to earn the MBA part time. All with a smile and positive step to pitch in and deliver to the customer.

Success and joy: Dave earned promotion into global program management and innovation leadership. Using his entrepreneurial blood he led global teams to deliver products in the USA, Europe, and Asia. He unified and coordinated the global teams so the products could be developed with a global design and launched simultaneously everywhere, training each sales force to deliver. The desire to learn and grow flourishes. Assignments in Asia were followed by program leadership in information management.

What Dave points at keeps happening. Dave keeps pointing.

Questions Answered

+   Why do people just want to fit in? To be liked? To give up and in
    to bullies?

A major part of any "I am..." is the desire to share and love. Connecting with others and sharing and loving is good. Being liked and fitting in when sharing with others is good and part of the connected "I am...." What is not good is that some people, the TTers and Takers, will use this tendency against people and appear false to people and try to get people in a Taker cycle. Never give in to this no matter how abusive the Takers become. Loving and sharing "I am..." people must learn how to deflect TTers and avoid Takers while showering them with love in one's heart and demonstrating how to share and connect in the spirit of "I am...." People want to control other people. Keep your own "I am...."

+   Why do I have to change? I like stability?

Nothing stays the same. Everything changes. People cannot stop change and live the same way they always have lived. Change will happen, so learn how to evolve and keep adding to receive joy through changing experiences. Trying to prevent change will lead to hurt as change will not stop.

+   What category do I fit in?

Never, ever fit into a category and give up your "I am..." which evolves as you evolve.

+   How can I tell the difference between constructive criticism and
    Turd Throwing?

Criticism is focused on having a dialogue to understand differences and similarities. The outcome from criticism is better understanding. But

TTers want to prevent difference and stop them, so little understanding comes from being stopped and hurt. Takers criticize to keep an "I am..." stuck in their Taker cycle working on the Taker problem.

+   How do I go to heaven?

Be your "I am...." Read spiritual texts like the Bible, the Koran and practice and pray to the Infinite "I am...." Above all, be joyful and loving in your experiences and share your joy and love.

Can I have sex and desire?

Base your life on morals and share your love, and your "I am..." will decide what is right for you.

+   How can I point and have experidigms without money?

Money is not needed to point up to your experidigm. Point and connect with others and you will begin to make the right choices for your experidigm.

+   How do I learn to experidigm?

Read *Choosing Up*. Really simple. Just picture something and take steps to create it, do it, and share it.

+   Why do people kill? Why do people have wars?

Mass delusion against differences and to protect and sever from these differences cause animosity. The delusion is created in the "you are..." mindset. Bad people make this delusion real to take and control.

+   I want to play the piano, but I cannot hear and see. Help?

Connect with someone who plays the piano, and play it with them. Beethoven became deaf and still wrote music.

+ Life is a kaleidoscope. Beautiful, but out of control and hard to understand. How do I understand?

Life has no meaning. Just go toward your experidigms.

+ Why-just why is life so…?

No answer to why life is just what it is. Chaos and change are life, not personal, so just flow with it.

+ Rites of passage?

Passage is an artificial experidigm, create your own experidigm. Life is like a bunch of jackhammers of different frequencies marching at you hard with changes, and more changes, all marching forward. Keep marching even through storms and tornadoes.

+ My mind is so confused, with so many thoughts. How do I gain control?

Do a simple act and share it. One small act at a time moves forward. No time line or goal. Just take a step, mental or physical and smile.

+ I sit on my couch. I have no inspiration. I want no one. Help?

Yes, sounds like a change hit you and knocked you down. Get up and out of your stagnant addiction. Point to an experidigm.

+ I do not like other people?

Connection is not about an emotion. Connection is about learning and making more selections.

+ I hurt, really hurt and nothing going right?

Go get a new experience and meet a new person. That is a start to getting smiles.

+   I cannot picture a good future? My pictures are bad.

Just get out and experience and pictures will come to you.

+   I lead the status quo and take and get all I want. Why should I give that up?

All the things in the world do not make your "I am...." One can live a "you are..." for their entire life and never really experience joy. Joy comes through the "I am...." Focus on joy, not on material acquisition.

+   So, I get abundance with my "I am..."?

The "I am..." is about joy and reaching you experidigms with connections. Joy is not necessarily abundance.

+   There is no God?

Wrong. The Infinite creates and connects through the "I am...ness." Maybe, just maybe, the Infinite looks through your senses, your eyes, your touch...

+   I am bad. I hurt people. I break laws. No one cares?

All of "I am...ness" cares. Unfortunately, amoral acts disconnect one from the Infinite and create isolation and stagnation. The cure is very simple – just begin loving - love each person and yourself, and your "I am...ness" will flourish and the bad will leave you as you focus on the NEXT experidigm. "I am..." people care.

+   I take what I want. Are you going to give to me, or else I enslave you?

The life of Takers is constant sadness, unfulfilled and unconnected, totally alone. Nothing is scarier than realizing one day one has intentionally chosen to be disconnected and alone.

Life is about sharing and connecting, not taking. If you take, you are well below the average of what life can give. You are near the bottom, but it might feel more than that when you take. Taking is at the bottom of life, even if you feel like you are "winning".

+ I am a TTer and have always been a TTer. My family were TTers. That is all we know. Am I evil?

Judging others leads down paths of disconnection, hurt and, hatred. No experidigm is real that hurts and harms another and is disconnected from other "I am…s." The TTer past can easily be overcome by loving and connecting with others on a simple love based experidigm.

+ I am part of my group and always have been. I do not want to connect with any others. Why should I?

Feeling safe and comfortable in one's situation may feel good, but that is not joy, and may be a delusion, living in stagnation or addiction, none of which is "I am…" fulfilling. Living only once in this space suit should encourage one to seek and share joy with the Infinite "I am…" as much as possible, and not waste any time.

+ I have nothing and when I point, I think I can, but why does nothing happen?

Actions and connections make it so, and the "I am…ness" opens up and shares. The art of moving forward is joyful as experience unfolds. Goal setting is different and fraught with frustration as unmet desires dominate the brain. Joy should dominate the brain. Choose joy and flow to the first action with a connected "I am…" group.

+ I have no time to think. What can I do?

Stop. Just stop and ask yourself: what experience would give you joy and with whom you can share and do it?

+ Why does life hurt so much?

Life keeps moving and changing. Life is impersonal. If you do not have an experidigm to focus upon and direct some actions to joy, then you are subject to an aimless life of blowing with the status quo winds being lost and confused. Life does not direct your life; free will directs life. Create an experidigm, point to it, connect with others and go. Life hurts if you let it direct and lead you.

+   How do I stop fearing?

Fearing is a delusion. Focus on creating a new experidigm and share.

+   Can I stop looking into the past and get free and move forward?

The past no longer exists. Only the present exists and no part of the past is here in the now unless you bring it with you. So think in the present and focus on moving forward to your experidigm.

+   How to stop giving my power away to others?

Read the books *TTers Beware* and *Avoid Takers*.

+   How can I share my success?

Listen to other experidigms and connect and share with them and assist them on realizing the actions to take to reach an experidigm. Or, get involved and create a group experidigm.

+   How can I perform miracles?

Religious history points to being connected to the Infinite "I am…ness" and receive wholeness above the mass delusion of the world. Love and sharing experidigms make miracles alive in the joy of the experidigm and overcomes the delusional "you are…" mind.

+   How can I love more?

Participate in an experidigm and share that and learn, and love will be transferred. Giving is not necessarily loving. Giving is good, but love is a connection with another on his or her path of life. Work on their and your path of life together. Like fireworks spreading across the sky, the experidigm spreads the love.

+   Why am I alone?

At any given moment, our past choices contain our free will, but our future choices open our free will now. If you choose connections, take the steps to connect.

The Ten Commandments from the NIV Bible – Verse 20 Exodus:

"And God spoke all these words:

[2] "I am the LORD your God, who brought you out of Egypt, out of the land of slavery.

[3] "You shall have no other gods before[a] me.

[4] "You shall not make for yourself an image in the form of anything in heaven above or on the earth beneath or in the waters below. [5] You shall not bow down to them or worship them; for I, the LORD your God, am a jealous God, punishing the children for the sin of the parents to the third and fourth generation of those who hate me, [6] but showing love to a thousand generations of those who love me and keep my commandments.

[7] "You shall not misuse the name of the LORD your God, for the LORD will not hold anyone guiltless who misuses his name.

[8] "Remember the Sabbath day by keeping it holy. [9] Six days you shall labor and do all your work, [10] but the seventh day is a Sabbath to the LORD your God. On it you shall not do any work, neither you, nor your son or

daughter, nor your male or female servant, nor your animals, nor any for-eigner residing in your towns. [11] For in six days the LORD made the heavens and the earth, the sea, and all that is in them, but he rested on the seventh day. Therefore the LORD blessed the Sabbath day and made it holy.

[12] "Honor your father and your mother, so that you may live long in the land the LORD your God is giving you.

[13] "You shall not murder.

[14] "You shall not commit adultery.

[15] "You shall not steal.

[16] "You shall not give false testimony against your neighbor.

[17] "You shall not covet your neighbor's house. You shall not covet your neighbor's wife, or his male or female servant, his ox or donkey, or any-thing that belongs to your neighbor."

Copy Editor

Special thanks to the sharp eye and wisdom of Maryann Errico. I learned so much and have a much greater respect for American English. Any grammar errors that remain in this work are there because I wanted to be creative, overriding Maryann and ignoring the built in word processor spell checker. Plus, I just want to make up new words, and that is Ok.

Illustrator

The beauty of illustrations is that they can contain words and all of our emo-tions together. Words may not be needed to describe them. Illustrations were created by two Italians: Federico Porto is an expert in seeing into my mind and taking exactly what I see and putting it on paper; Sonja Monaca simplifies to show the "I am…" essence of the idea. I am grateful to Maurizio DeAscanis who devoted his bilingual skills to unite me with illustrators and translate our discussions.

Endnotes

1 The NIV Study Bible 10th Anniversary Edition. 1984. The Zondervan Corporation. Genesis 3:1-24

2 Myers, Isabel Briggs & Peter B. 1995. *Gifts differing: understanding personality type.* Mountain View, CA: Davies-Black Publishing. <u>ISBN 0-89106-074-X</u>.

3 Maslow, A. 1954. *Motivation and personality.* New York, NY: Harper. *ISBN 0-06-041987-3*

4 Ovid's narrative poem Metamorphoses

5 Freud, Sigmund. 1949. *The Ego and the Id.* The Hogarth Press Ltd. London

6 Frankl, Victor. 1946 *Man's Search for Meaning.* Vienna, Austria, ⊠Verlag für Jugend und Volk (Austria)

7 The NIV Study Bible 10th Anniversary Edition. 1984. The Zondervan Corporation. Book of Ecclesiastes

8 The NIV Study Bible 10th Anniversary Edition. 1984. The Zondervan Corporation. Book of Ecclesiastes

9 Bejan, Adrian and Zane, J. Peder. 2012 *Design in Nature: How the Constructal Law governs evolution in Biology, Physics, Technology and Social Organizations.* ISBN 978-0307744340.

10 Hill, Napoleon. 1937. *Think and Grow Rich*. The Raston Society ISBN 978-1-604—59-187-3

11 McTaggart, Lynne. 2003 *The Field: Quest for the Secret Force of the Universe* ISBN 0-06-093117-5

12 The NIV Study Bible 10th Anniversary Edition. 1984. The Zondervan Corporation. Book of Ecclesiastes